NIAGARA STORY
VOLUME 4
THE CANADIANS

BY
ROBERT J. FOLEY

ILLUSTRATED
BY
GEORGE BALBAR

THE HAUNTED PRESS
NIAGARA FALLS, ONTARIO

ISBN: 1-895528-03-8

Foley, Robert J. 1941-
Niagara Story Volume 4
The Canadians
by Robert J. Foley
Includes index

Illustrated by:
Balbar, George 1930-

The Haunted Press,
A Division of 314340 Ontario Limited
4219 Briarwood Avenue,
Niagara Falls, Ontario
L2E 6Z1

Printed in Canada by: Peninsula Press Limited, St. Catharines, Ontario

Bound in Canada by: John Van Huizen Book Binding, St. Catharines, Ontario

Canadian Cataloguing in Publication Data

Foley, Robert J., 1941-
    Niagara Story

Includes index
Contents: v. 1. Beginnings — v. 2. The War of 1812 — v. 3. The Welland Canal.
v. 4. The Canadians.
ISBN 1-895528-00-3 (v. 1) ISBN 1-895528-02-X (v. 2) ISBN 1-895528-01-1 (v. 3)
ISBN 1-895528-03-8

1. Niagara Peninsula (Ont.) - History. I. Title.

FC3093.N5F64 1994   971.3'38   C94-900997-0
F1059.N5F64 1994

Dedicated
To
My Mother
Bernie Auger
Who raised and nurtured me
&
My mother-in-law
Isabel Cairney
Who welcomed me into her family 27 years ago

The Entire Niagara Story Series
is Respectfully
Dedicated to
George and Olive Seibel

CONTENTS

CHAPTER ONE

AT ONE WITH THE LAND

Throughout the history of the Niagara Peninsula religion has played a prominent role in the evolution of the various communities that have called it home. When we think of religion, the picture of the Methodist circuit rider or the preacher waving his bible from the pulpit usually comes to mind. However, the Neutral Indians who settled here about seven hundred years ago were also a deeply religious people.

The mythology of the Iroquois, which took their roots from the Neutrals, showed a complexity previously seen only in the civilization of Iran. The world was seen as the battlefield of two hostile powers, light and darkness, good and evil, high and low. This dualism was absent from the beliefs of other northern peoples.

The Iroquoian people believe that terrestrial phenomena possess prototypes of all living things. These prototypes (ongwe) have always existed and are immortal. They live on the side of the dome of heaven, which we cannot see. Deer, Bear, Duck, Wind Who Moves About from Place to Place, Daylight, Night, Thick Night, Star, Maize, Wolf, Medicine, Fire Dragon with the Body of Pure White Colour, and the Aurora Borealis are among these ongwe. Their houses are generally long with the sleeping mats at each end. In the morning they go hunting and return in the evening.

Like the Judeo-Christian tradition the Iroquoian people had their creation story, which sheds some light on the dualistic nature of their faith. This is how the Iroquois relate the development of the world: **In the celestial village there once lived a couple whose daughter Awenhai (fruitful earth) offered her hand in marriage to the celestial chief. The hut of this chief, the most exalted member of the exalted community of ongwe, stood in a wide field under the tree Onodja. The blossoms of this tree gave forth the celestial light; in that world above the sky there was no sun.**

The chief accepted the maiden's offer and married her. But before he and Awenhai had ever slept together, he made her pregnant with his breath. No one had any idea that this could happen, and the chief became so jealous that he caused the tree of light, Onodja, to be uprooted, thus leaving a gaping hole in the canopy of heaven through which he hurled his wife together with Maize, Bean, Sunflower, Tobacco, Deer, Wolf, Bear, and Beaver, and all their relations. There then appeared the terrestrial forms known to us, but the immortal ongwe nevertheless continue to exist in heaven. Then the tree Onodja was set up again and the hole closed. This ended the first phase of the cosmic drama.

Meanwhile Awenhai fell towards a light blue speck, which she realized was an endless sea with many sea birds on it. No earth was anywhere to be seen. The animals saw her fall and called on Great Turtle to carry her. Muskrat brought earth up from the seabed and spread it out on the shell of the turtle resulting in an island. At the same time the birds flew up and caught Awenhai and set her down on the turtle's back.

The earth grew quickly; bushes, grass and other plants sprang up. After two nights Awenhai found a deer

carcass and a little fire, so that she prepared a meal. Eventually she gave birth to a girl child. This was the first daughter from whom all Iroquois are descended. Jikonsaseh, The descendant of this first daughter, held a special place in the life of the Iroquoian language group of tribes that included the Hurons and the Neutrals. She was the "Mother of Nations" or "Peace Queen," who ruled over the league and non-league Iroquoians alike. The eldest daughter would succeed her mother in this role.

The daughter of Awenhai was also magically impregnated and gave birth to twin sons, Great Spirit and Evil Spirit. She died giving birth to the latter. Great Spirit fashioned the sun from her head, from her body the moon and stars. He then made the seas, the rivers, the mountains and valleys, and finally human beings. Evil Spirit worked too and from him came anger, strife and warfare. Obviously two such opposites could not live together and so they fought for two days and Evil Spirit was defeated and sent into exile in the netherworld, but his work remains behind to plague the children of the earth.

The Iroquois world was filled with spirits and earthly symbols of them were everywhere. Diseases were caused by demonlike spirits called False Faces. Fortunately these could be harnessed to affect a cure. The False Face Society was one of the best known Iroquoian Religious Societies. They were concerned with the cure of diseases especially of the head, shoulders and limbs. A headache, toothache or swollen ankle and the like were all conditions ministered to by the False Face Society.

False Face members wore elaborate

masks, which were endowed with curative powers. By wearing the mask and performing the proper rituals these powers were given to the members who ministered to the sick. When called upon the members would appear at the longhouse of the patient. Usually the sick person summoned the False Faces after a dream in which they appeared. Dawning their masked they formed a circle around the patient. Some members danced and shook their rattles, usually made from turtle shells, others scooped up glowing embers from the fire and blew ashes at the sick person. Once cured the patient himself automatically became a member of the society. He then procured his own mask who's design usually came from the dream, which prompted the summoning of the False Faces to his aid.

The Iroquois held religious festivals throughout the year to thank Great Spirit. The Green Corn Festival in late summer was in thanksgiving for corn, the Harvest (October), Rise of the Maple (February or March according to sap levels), and the Strawberry, first fruit of the season (June). All gave thanks for the bounty of the land. The Ceremonial of Midwinter ushering in the new year (usually late January or early February) lasted a week and concerned itself with dreams, confession and thanksgiving. It was the time when new babies born since the Green Corn Festival four months earlier were named. The Iroquoian people were one with the land and their religious practices reflected that oneness.

PIONEER FAITH

The first Christian presents in the Niagara Peninsula occurred in the winter of 1626-27. The French Recollect missionary Joseph de la Roche Daillon wintered among the Neutrals. He described the land in this way: "This Country is incomparably larger, more beautiful, and better than any of these countries....There are an incredible number of stags...and other animals....A stay there is quite recreating and convenient; the rivers furnish much excellent fish; the earth gives good grain, more than is needed. They have squash, beans, and other vegetables in abundance."

Daillon was met in the peninsula with hostility due to the stories related to them by the Hurons who feared that the French might upset the delicate balance that kept the Neutrals out of the wars fought between themselves and the Iroquois Confederacy.

The two Jesuit missionaries Brebeuf and Chaumonot met similar resistance in 1640. Their peace gifts were refused by the Neutrals, who declared, "do you not know ... the danger in which you are putting the country?" Again that delicate position of the Neutrals prevented any penetration by the Christian missions.

With the dispersal of the Neutrals in 1652 the peninsula remained empty of human habitation for some one hundred and thirty years except for a small outpost at Fort Erie. The French explorer LaSalle visited the area in 1678 with his party that included Father Louis Hennepin. Most of LaSalle's activities were confined to the east or American side of the river, however, the tradition is that Hennepin celebrated the first Mass in Niagara at a site overlooking the falls. Legend places this site at Fallsview where the Shrine of Our Lady of Peace stands today.

With the outbreak of the American Revolution loyalist refugees began to pour into the area of Fort Niagara. In 1781 a number of families crossed the Niagara to clear the land and begin a new life in the wilderness that was the Niagara Peninsula. Of course they brought their Christian faith with them.

Because the American colonies had been a haven for nonconformists from England and persecuted religious minorities from across Europe, the mix of denominations that settled here, was great. Besides the official church,

settled here was great. Besides the official church, the Church of England, there were a great number of Presbyterians and Methodists, with a sprinkling of Baptists thrown in for good measure.

One of the first places of worship in the area was built at Stamford in 1791. The Presbyterian Meeting House was built from white oak timbers covered with clapboard. Stamford Presbyterian Church on St. Paul Street in Niagara Falls stands on the site today.

The first ecumenical movement in Niagara took place in 1795 when the Anglicans, Methodists, and Baptists along with a few families of Quakers and Lutherans built a log church on Lundy's Lane near Portage Road. This nondenominational church served, not only as a place of worship, but as the first school in that part of the township. This meeting house was in the middle of the Battle of Lundy's Lane and was seriously damaged. Drummond Hill Presbyterian Church is located near the site today.

The Anglicans did not get there first church in Stamford until 1825. The Lieu-

tenant Governor, Sir Pereguine Maitland, began spending the summer at Stamford Park, his summer home on the brow of the escarpment. His wife wanted a church closer than Chippawa or Queenston and the land for the building of St. John's was donated by Captain Robert Dee, an aide to Maitland. The deed was dated September 20, 1820. The church was consecrated by the Lord Bishop of Quebec on September 28, 1825.

Despite the outward signs of cooperation between the various Protestant denominations there were points of contention and friction in the community. John Graves Simcoe was anxious to have the Church of England recognized as the official church of Upper Canada. To this end one seventh of the land in a township was reserved for the Anglican clergy. By the Marriage Act of 1793 only members of the official church could perform marriage ceremonies. This caused an uproar among the other clergy. The one exception to the Anglican Clergy rule was that if you were more than eighteen miles from an Anglican clergyman a justice of the peace was duly authorized to perform the ceremony. One story is told of a couple of a persuasion other than Anglican who went to be married by the justice of the peace only to discover that they were only sixteen miles from the clergyman of the district. Being law abiding citizens they trekked two miles into the woods and, standing on a convenient log, the J.P. solemnized the union. In 1798 the act was amended to include the clergy of the Lutheran, Calvinist and Church of Scotland (Presbyterian), but that still left the Methodists, Roman Catholics and other denominations out in the cold. Despite the constant uproar it was not until 1831 that the act was amended to include all clergy.

The Methodists were served mainly by itinerant preachers in those early days. The Methodist Niagara Circuit was established in 1795 with Darius Dunham as circuit rider, a preacher who would travel by horseback from one area to another holding meetings in peoples homes. He appointed Christian Warner as the Niagara Circuit Recording Steward. It was his job to attend quarterly meetings and collect any money that his classes were prepared to donate to the circuit rider. Any funds left over were saved up for the building of a church. The Warner church was built below the escarpment just west of St. Davids in 1801. Colonel John Butler began agitating for an Anglican clergyman shortly after the settlement of the area and in 1792, with the help of Robert Hamilton of Queenston, the Society for the Propagation of the Gospel in Foreign Parts sent the Reverend Robert Addison to Newark (N.O.T.L.). Addison began by holding services in his home until the completion of St. Mark's. He traveled to Queenston and other communities to serve the official church.

Despite the differences the early pioneers worked and worshipped in relative harmony.

THE CHURCHES OF ST. CATHARINES

We begin our look at the churches of St. Catharines by relating an interesting story referred to by Dr. John N. Jackson in his book, "St. Catharines Ontario, Its Early Years." The story, taken from the "Centennial Souvenir: Church of St. Catherine of Alexandria (St. Catharines), 1945," tells of the dedication of the church in 1845 and how St. Catherine came to be its patron. Dr. Jackson quoted from the souvenir: "In the year 1679 de la Salle, with a small party, was portaging from Lake Ontio (Lake Ontario) to the Lake of the Eries (Lake Erie) and was following a route up a creek some four leagues (12 miles) west of the Niagara River. . . . After two days of awful toil the voyageurs reached a spot where now lays Oak Hill Park . . . and camped by a never failing spring. They rested there for a day and Pere Hennepin, being with the party, solemnized his daily Mass. It was the feast day of St. Catherine, so the good father blessed the spring and called it St. Catherine's Well."

Although no documentary evidence is available Dr. Jackson concludes that the story could be true. If so then Father Hennepin celebrated the first Christian service on the Twelve Mile Creek.

The first permanent church was established at St. Catharines in 1796. Robert Hamilton, the prominent merchant from Queenston, deeded the land to the church wardens of Grantham Township, John Gould and Abel Letten. There may have been a small meeting house of the Church of England at St. Catharines from 1791 to the completion of the new church. The building, a small wooden structure 30 feet by 40 feet, was used by several denominations in those early years. It had a small cemetery attached to it, which was closed after a cholera epidemic in the 1830s.

The church was built on the corner of

Yates Street and St. Paul. It lay close to the crossing place on the Twelve and was the only church in St. Catharines until 1823. In 1835 it was sold to the Wesleyans who used it until it burned down in 1836.

This was the first Anglican Church built outside of Niagara, the main centre of commerce and government business in the area. Because of the laws governing marriage people had to travel to Niagara until this church was completed.

In 1823 Jonathan Clendennan sold a lot on St. Paul Street to the Methodist trustees for ten pounds to build their church. St. Paul Street United stands near the spot where this initial Methodist church was situated. It became known as the mother church of Methodism in Niagara. From it was developed a preaching circuit in 1832, which took in the communities that sprang up along the canal at Thorold and Allanburg as well as the established settlements at St. John's and Beaverdams.

In 1834 a flurry of building activity began on Academy Street (Church Street). The Presbyterians, with the help of Oliver Phelps, the contractor who built the wooden locks for the first canal, started their church. Until its completion they met at Phelps' Red Mill on Geneva Street. The corner stone for St. Georges Anglican Church was laid in 1835 on Academy Street.

In 1844 the Scottish Presbyterians built their church on Centre Street. The Baptists completed a stone church on Queen Street.

Although the first Christian service in St. Catharines was celebrated by a Roman Catholic priest, the few Catholics in the area were ministered to by priests who came into the area to service the military through the 1820s.

The first Catholic Church in the Niagara Peninsula, St. Vincent de Paul, was built at Niagara-on-the-Lake in 1826. A mission was established at Fallsview in 1837 called St. Edwards. Its name was eventually changed to Our Lady of Peace in the 1860s. The parish priest from St. Vincent's used to ride from one community to the next much as the Methodist circuit riders did.

The influx of Irish labourers on the Welland Canal beginning in 1824 made the building of a permanent facility in St. Catharines a viable project. A wooden church was erected in 1834 to serve the Irish labourers and the pastor, Father Constantine Lee, was instrumental in keeping the various factions within the community at peace even if it were an armed peace.

The St. Catharines Journal of March 31, 1842 reported the observations of a visitor this way: "This village is well furnished with places of worship. From the conspicuous position of three of them, placed on one street, on the western side of the village, strangers might be disposed to think the inhabitants a very religious community.. . . The Catholic, Episcopalian and Presbyterian churches are on Academy Street, and are neat structures, the two former, surmounted with towers or spires; and considerable taste is displayed on the Episcopalian meeting house and tower."

Tragedy visited the Irish twice in 1843. Their indefatigable pastor died of pneumonia after traveling to a dying parishioner in a winter rainstorm in January and their little church burned to the ground on August 23rd of the same year. Their new pastor, Father W.P. McDonagh, wasted no time in beginning a campaign to replace the loss. The new church was literally built by the Irish labourers on the Welland Canal. With the help of the local business community the corner stone was laid and on June 10, 1844 the first Mass was celebrated with 2000 people spilling into the street to listen to the service.

In 1959 the Church of St. Catherine of Alexandria became the Cathedral Church of the new Diocese of St. Catharines. Today the spiritual diversity of St. Catharines can be seen by the proliferation of churches, mosques and temples throughout the city. It is a credit to our community that, despite this diversity, we are able to live in harmony.

CHAPTER TWO
GETTING AROUND NIAGARA

FOREST HIGHWAYS

Before the coming of Europeans to North America a vast trading network crisscrossed the continent moving a variety of goods from as far south as the Gulf of Mexico, from the Arctic Circle, from the great plains and from the east coast to the Niagara Peninsula. Some commodities passed through several tribes before reaching their eventual destination. For example the Algonkins might be the origin of furs that eventually ended up in the Carolinas, but to get there they would have to pass through the Hurons, Neutrals, Iroquois and the Susquehannocks. Conversely Gourds for oil would come through the network from that end. The Algonkins traded meat, fish, furs and birch-bark canoes to the Hurons for shells, gourds and corn. Through the Neutrals some Algonkin goods would end up with the Hurons perennial enemies, the Iroquois. The Algonkin birch-bark canoe was very popular with them. The Neutrals acted as the middlemen in the trade between these enemies allowing the movement of goods that each needed.

To accomplish the trade in the wilderness goods had to be moved over great distances. In Ontario and New York State water transport became the quickest and easiest way to get around. The canoe was the mainstay of Indian transportation. Birch-bark was the best material because it was light and easily carried over the many portages necessary in a long journey. Unfortunately birch in any quantity grew in the north country of the Algonkins and the Iroquois had no supply to draw from. Iroquois canoes were usually made from a single pine log that was hollowed out. these proved to be too heavy to carry

and became quickly waterlogged.

As we have seen the Iroquois preferred to trade for the much lighter birch-bark canoes.

The Algonkin skill at canoe making was known throughout the northeast. Canoes were usually made in early summer when the bark was more easily harvested. The builder would first select a suitable tree. His next problem was climbing the smooth trunk up to the point where the good bark ended. To assist him in his climb he tied a strong leather tong about twelve inches long to each of his big toes. This gave him traction much as a lumberjacks spikes do today. He next took a sharp pointed knife and cut a small strip of bark from around the trunk. Sliding down he cut a straight line to the bottom. Two helpers usually held the bark in place with light poles until it could be gently lowered to the ground. The bark was then heated to flatten it out and weighted down to hold it in place.

The builder next cut cedar slats, which were used as ribs to add strength to the canoe. Holes were punched in the bark with a sharp piece of bone and the fine roots of a fir tree was used to sow the bark together.

The women also had a role to play in this enterprise. While the men busied themselves with the actual construction the women chewed pine gum to make it soft. The gum was then heated and used as a sealant on the seams of the canoe. One canoe took about two weeks to complete. Although birch-bark was the material of choice sometimes spruce bark, elm bark or moose hides were used.

Canoes came in several sizes from a small two man to one that could accommodate as many as fourteen paddlers. The canoe was normally paddled from the kneeling position, however, an expert could

stand in the stern and maneuver a large craft through a rapids. Where the rapids were too dangerous to shoot and the water was deep enough along the banks the canoe was pulled along by men on shore. Where that was not possible the canoe was unloaded and two men carried it upside down over their heads while the others transported the cargo.

Although water was the preferred mode of transportation, trade goods were also carried over an elaborate trail system that developed throughout this part of the continent. Because it was the port of trade all trails led to the Niagara Peninsula. Like our modern highway system the Indians had there arterial trails, other major trails and some back trails. These trails were also signed so a traveler knew what trail he was following. Saplings were bent to grow in certain shapes and each trail had its own particular design.

The arterial trail that ran through the peninsula was the Iroquois Trail. It began in New York State and crossed the Niagara River at present day Queenston. Passing through St. Davids and St. Catharines it followed a route along the bottom of the escarpment to Hamilton. Here it cut west through Ancaster and Brantford all the way the Detroit frontier. A major trail branched off from the Iroquois at St. Davids called the Mohawk Trail. This route cut through the Short Hills before running parallel to the Iroquois along the top of the escarpment. It intersected with the Iroquois Trail at Ancaster. Another major trail branched off from the Mohawk just north of the Short Hills and followed Twenty Mile Creek. It rejoined the Mohawk just before its junction with the Iroquois.

A trail ran from the mouth of the Niagara River along the shore of Lake Ontario all the way to the Ottawa River. In the southern peninsula a trail ran from Fort Erie along the lake shore to the Grand River. From the mouth of the Grand it followed the river until it also joined up with the Iroquois Trail east of Brantford. A trail from Chippawa intersected with this trail near Dunnville. All these trails were linked by secondary trails along their routes.

Besides trade these trails were also used by hunters in their far ranging search for game. War parties could often be seen moving down the trails as they raided their enemies for prisoners and booty.

Most of the highways we use today follow the track of these early Indian trails. The Iroquois Trail west of Hamilton is now the 401. The Mohawk follows Lundy's Lane and Beaverdams Road before becoming old Highway #8 now Regional Road #81.

Some foggy evening as you drive some of our Heritage Highways don't be surprised if the ghosts of Warriors come trotting out of the mist.

CANOES & WAGON WHEELS

With the arrival of the Europeans and their pursuit of the fur trade, transportation in the New World began to evolve. The trade relied heavily on the canoe, but the traders were constantly attempting to find more efficient ways to carry larger payloads over longer distances.

When LaSalle reached the Niagara in 1679 he found the Falls of Niagara standing in the way of his route to the upper lakes. He used the ancient Indian portage from the Landing (Lewiston, N.Y.) to a point above the falls opposite the mouth of the Chippawa. LaSalle saw the potential for use of a sailing vessel on the upper lakes and laid the keel of the Barque Griffon on January 22, 1679 in the mouth of Cayuga Creek. The Griffon set sail that spring with trade goods but never returned. Speculation has ranged from a ship wreck to its deliberate destruction by the Ottawas who viewed it as a threat to their position in the fur trade on the upper lakes.

Despite minor successes in improving the transportation the canoe remained king in the upper lakes trading area. In a letter written in May of 1726 Longueuil observed, "100 English at the portage of the River Oswego with more than 60 canoes. . . . He has seen in his voyage more than 100 Indian canoes, which carried furs to the English to exchange for "L'eau de vie." He has also met many canoes of Nipissing and Saulteur Indians coming from Lake Huron to trade with the English."

After 1680 the canoes became bigger to accommodate more freight. The larger canoes were called Canot du Maitre and were used for the long haul from Montreal to Grand Portage on Lake Superior. For the inland trade a smaller canoe, the "Canot du Nord" was used as fewer men were needed to paddle and portage around the numerous rapids. This canoe was 24 feet long, 4 1\2 feet wide and 20 inches deep with a crew of four. The Canot du Maitre was 35 feet long, 4 1/2 feet wide and 30 inches deep. It carried a crew of eight plus the clerk and took 26 days to reach Michilimackinac from Montreal. The typical load carried by the Canot du Maitre was 5500 lbs of freight plus 9 men and provisions weighing another 2800 lbs for a total of 8300 lbs. It is amazing that such a frail craft could handle over four tons. It is no wonder that they rarely lasted two years and most were done in one season.

When the British defeated the French in 1760 they took over the northern fur trade as well. In October, 1784 the canoe's importance was reinforced in a report from the Frobisher brothers to General Haldimand: "The Inland Navigation from Montreal, by which the North-West business is carried on, is perhaps the most extensive of any in the known world, but is only practicable for canoes on account of the great number of Carrying Places."

Canoe building became quite an industry. They were manufactured at Trois Riviere, at the Island of St. Joseph near Michilimackinac

and at Grand Portage where upwards of seventy canoes were built on contract in one season.

To hasten the trip on the upper lakes larger sailing ships were built. The Northwest Company had two vessels of 12 and 15 tons on Lake Superior in 1790. In 1793 the company had the 45 ton Beaver and the 40 ton Athabaska plying the route from Detroit to the Sault. The Athabaska had been floated down the Sault Rapids from Lake Superior that spring. A bigger ship, the Otter of 75 tons replaced her on Superior. In 1803 the Otter was reported to carry 95 tons of freight from the Sault to Grand Portage and made four or five trips in a season.

From the earliest time Niagara was a main cog in fur trade transportation. With the impending loss of the east bank of the Niagara River the British set up a new portage on the west bank in 1790. Goods destined for the northwest were off loaded at the Queenston dock and transported the 17.7km to Chippawa where they were loaded onto another vessel for the trip through the upper lakes.

The movement of goods over the Portage Road was done on a contract basis. There were two bidders for the franchise, Robert Hamilton of Queenston headed a syndicate made up of George Forsythe, John Burch and Archibald Cunningham. The other bidder was Philip Stedman Jr. of the east bank who owned land around the American Falls. He moved his cattle to the west bank and established a farm near Black Creek to raise oxen for the job. He promised to have equipment enough to carry 10 tons of freight plus an extra wagon capable of carrying two tons of bulk cargo.

Unlike the Stedman's the Hamilton group planned to use local farmers with their wagons to transport goods over the portage. They had been doing this since 1788 and it gave the farmers a much needed supplement to their income. Much to their relief the Hamilton syndicate won the contract.

It was not just freight wagons that used the Portage Road. A regular stagecoach service developed between Niagara on the Lake and Chippawa with a stop in Queenston.

Two lines began operation in 1798. One by John Fanning, a hotel operator from Chippawa and the other by J. Fairbanks, another Chippawa hotel owner, and T. Hind. An advertisement, which ran in the Upper Canada Gazette may be of some interest: **"J. Fairbanks and Thomas Hind acquaint friends and the public that their stagecoach will continue to run between Newark and Chippawa on Mondays, Wednesdays and Fridays; to start from Newark at 7 A.M. on each day and return the same evening, provided four passengers take seats by 4 in the afternoon. Otherwise to start from Chippawa at 7 o'clock the following morning and returning the same evening. Each passenger is allowed fourteen pounds of baggage, and to pay one dollar. Way passengers to be picked up at sixpence a mile York currency. Good horses and careful drivers are provided and that attention and dispatch which are necessary to the ease, satisfaction and convenience of the passengers may always be expected. Letters fourpence each."**

Fanning won either way. If the coach had its four passengers his equipment was running and the fares paid. If the coach was held overnight the waiting passengers were put up at his hotel.

Shortly after the War of 1812 steam came along and the idea of the Welland Canal was born changing transportation forever.

THE CORDUROY ROAD

Although water transportation remained the fastest and easiest way to travel in early Upper Canada, roads began to be built as the Loyalists settled the land. We have already discussed the Niagara Portage Road that skirted the falls and the Indian trails that criss crossed the Peninsula, however, there were a number of other projects that had far reaching affects on the growth of this part of Ontario.

When Upper Canada was formed in 1791 road building began in earnest. Prior to that an "express" ran from Montreal each winter through the various communities finishing up in Detroit. This express consisted of one man with a couple of Indian guides and carried mail for the troops and merchants. They traveled by snowshoe following the lakeshore and rivers making just one trip a season. It became obvious that if the province was to prosper it needed better communications during the winter months when the lakes were frozen.

The first major project in Upper Canada was started by John Graves Simcoe in 1796. He envisioned roads much like those the Romans had built in England; long and straight to carry troops quickly to any trouble spot. Yonge Street was to be the link between York, his capital, and Lake Simcoe with its link to the upper lakes. Augustus Jones partially surveyed the route in 1794, but it was only blazed part way. It was left to the settlers to improve the road as needed. In December 1795 Simcoe ordered the route completed and in January 1796 the Queen's Rangers, Simcoe's old regiment, began working. They pushed the road through to Lake Simcoe in six weeks.

His other project was Dundas Street that was to run from Detroit to the Quebec border. This road was completed from Kingston to Ancaster in 1800.

Government funding for road construction was meager and apart from the two trunk lines road construction and maintenance was left to the local population. In the Niagara Peninsula one of the most pressing problems was the Black Swamp that covered some two miles between Niagara and the head of Lake Ontario. Commerce was often totally cut off during the spring and times of thaw in winter. A causeway was proposed, however, estimates of thousands of dollars and months of labour made the job seem impossible. This did not deter the locals from launching a

campaign to raise the necessary funds and labour. Handbills were posted at taverns and mills stating: "those gentlemen who are inclined to aid so necessary a work will have an opportunity of adding their donations." Construction began almost immediately.

The problem proved less formidable than predicted and after five weeks the job was two-thirds completed. A notice in a local paper announced: "Three hundred and sixty dollars more, gentlemen, and the work will be completed." The project was finished in record time and the link with the head of the lake completed.

However, this was a good news-bad news situation. The good news was the road was finished; the bad news was that it was an infamous corduroy road. The only way to bridge swampy ground in those days was to build a corduroy road. When wet ground was reached the trees that had to be cut down were laid at right angles to the path of the road side by side. Earth was spread over them to smooth out the surface. In theory this provided a dry relatively easy ride over

swampy ground. The reality was that the earth packed on top soon disappeared under the combined traffic and rain leaving a wash board effect similar to those found on gravel roads today after long periods of rain. To add to the problem logs were not of uniform size. A log two feet in diameter might find itself partnered with another just one foot in diameter. It is not hard to imagine the rough ride that one would experience. In many instances the log surface would decay quickly giving way suddenly under the weight of a carriage or wagon. Conscientious drivers often led their horses over the corduroy portion to avoid having them step into a crack coming up lame or worse.

If the local builders had the time and resources they would split the logs leaving the flat side up. this helped, however, even the maintained roads quickly deteriorated under the onslaught of rain and frost.

Some of the comments of the travelers of the day may shed some light on the conditions encountered. Anna Jameson recorded these observations in 1837: "The road was scarcely passable; there were no longer cheerful farms and clearings, but the dark pine forest and rank swamp, crossed by the terrific corduroy paths, (my bones ache at the mere recollection!), . . . I set my teeth, screwed myself to my seat, and commended myself to Heaven-but I was well-nigh dislocated!

At length I abandon my seat altogether, and made an attempt to recline on the straw at the bottom of the cart, disposing my cloaks, carpet-bags, and pillow so as to afford some support-but all in vain; myself and all my well-contrived edifice of comfort were pitched hither and thither, and I expected at every moment to be thrown over headlong."

C.R. Weld wrote in 1850: "Resuming our drive we entered the bush, now unenlivened by settlements, their absence being made painfully sensible to us by the terrible condition of the road. Holes masked by mud were of constant occurrence. Into these our vehicle plunged with a crash, threatening to reduce it to atoms; but, much to my surprise, it was on each occasion dragged out by the willing horses, apparently uninjured. Worse, however, than the holes, was the dreadful corduroy composed of large logs, over which we bumped with a dislocatory motion, rendering it difficult to keep one's seat."

Perhaps the poem by Carrie Munson Hoople best sums it up:
Half a log, half a log,
  Half a log onward,
Shaken and out of breath,
  Rode we and wondered.
Ours not to reason why,
  Ours but to clutch and cry
While onward we thundered.

ALL ABOARD!

Next to the Welland Canal the most important development in the growth of the Niagara Peninsula from Suspension Bridge (Niagara Falls, N.Y.) to Hamilton opened. The Great Western was the coming of the steam rail-

British North America was slow to enter the steam era. The first steam engine was built in England in 1829 and the first in North America was built at New York in 1830. By 1840 there were 2,800 miles of track in the United States, which rose to 9,000 miles by 1850. At the same time there was less than 70 miles of track in all of British North America.

The first railroad in Upper Canada, the Erie & Ontario, was chartered in 1835. It ran a horse drawn railway from Chippawa to Queenston. An 1842 timetable gives us an idea of how the operation worked: "The cars leave Chippawa for Queenston daily, in time to arrive there for the Toronto steamer, (the Transit), at twelve o'clock; reaching Chippawa on return, about 2 p.m., where a steamer will be in readiness to carry travellers on to Buffalo."

The fare was $1.00, which included the steamer to Buffalo. The connections at both ends of the line allowed passengers to travel from Toronto to Buffalo in the same day.

The problem with the E.& O. was that it was a seasonal operation and although it carried freight it could not compete with the canal. It was rescued in 1852 by a revision to its charter, which allowed it to vary it's route to parallel the Great Western at the suspension bridge. It rebuilt the line to accommodate steam and reopened in 1854. It had stations at Chippawa, Clifton, Elgin, St. Davids, Queenston and Niagara each with freight and passenger facilities. As with the Erie & Ontario it linked up with Davids, Queenston and Niagara each with freight and passenger facilities. As with the Erie & Ontario it linked up with steamships to send travellers into the vast world beyond the peninsula.

If Upper Canada was slow to adopt the steam engine it pushed forward with vigor when it did. In 1851 only the Toronto, Simcoe and Lake Huron Union Rail Road was running with the Great Western under con-

struction. In 1853 the Great Western line

Railway had its beginnings in 1834 with the charter of the London & Gore Railroad Company. Its mandate was to provide service from Burlington to London and Lake Huron. Several factors prevented this road from materializing, however, it remained an active company resulting in a name change in 1845 to the Great Western Railroad Company. The 1845 Act also expanded its mandate as stated: "the said company shall have full power to make or continue their Rail-Road, from the town of London to Point Edward, at the foot of Lake Huron, and to the Detroit River, and any point of the Niagara River."

The Great Western moved its eastern terminal to Niagara Falls in 1853 to take advantage of the new suspension bridge across the Niagara. This move brought towns and villages such as St. Catharines, Thorold, Merritton, Grimsby and Beamsville into the main stream of the continent wide rail system.

In 1847 the surveying work began and an early completion and the resultant economic boom looked promising. However, financial problems intervened and it was 1852 before construction got underway in earnest. Work between Niagara Falls and St. Catharines was boosted by two steam excavators to help with the heavy jobs needed. Several bridges had to be built including those to cross the Twenty, Sixteen, Fifteen, Twelve and Ten Mile Creeks. The Bridges over the Twenty and Sixteen Mile Creeks were described as follows: " The Bridge to be erected over the Twenty Mile Creek will be 1200 feet in length and 60 feet high and the bridge over the Sixteen Mile Creek 800 feet in length and of the same height."

The line was opened on November 1, 1853 with an inaugural run from Hamilton to Suspension Bridge. All went well until the train passed through the deep cut Between St. Davids and Thorold. The track here was newly laid and dropped in the soft clay as the locomotive passed over it. The front of the engine derailed breaking the coupling. The passengers walked the six miles to Suspension Bridge. Despite this accident regular service was instituted on November 10th and in January 1854 the through train between Niagara Falls and Windsor made its first run.

In 1856 a charter was issued for the Port Dalhousie and Thorold Railway to run service between these two points. In 1857 the name was changed to the Welland Railway and ran from Port Dalhousie to Port Colborne to carry freight off loaded from ships too heavy to enter the locks of the Welland Canal.

By 1857 the "Canada Directory" showed the following: The Buffalo & Lake Huron Railroad running from Fort Erie to Goderich with 114 miles of track with 46 miles still under construction; The Great Western from Suspension Bridge to Windsor; the Welland Railroad from Port Dalhousie to Port Colborne; and the Woodstock & Lake Erie , which was chartered but not yet operational, to run from Suspension bridge to Woodstock.

William Hamilton Merritt opposed the Erie & Ontario Railroad in 1833 and managed to delay its charter for two years. However, once the canal was through to Lake Erie he became a proponent of rail travel. In 1836 he was approached by the Niagara & Detroit Rivers Railroad to promote a line from Sandwich to Fort Erie. This line was long in coming due to opposition from the Great Western to a southern route to the Detroit River. The plans lay in limbo until William Thompson of Queenston purchased the Erie & Ontario in 1863. He had incorporated the Fort Erie Railroad Company in 1857. He incorporated the Erie & Niagara Extension Railway Company in 1868 to build a line from Fort Erie to Windsor. This company became the Canada Southern in 1869.

The Great Western fought the new line vigorously as did the northern communities. This was a shorter route to Detroit than the northern route and the Great Western feared the competition. This time the new railroad won out. Leaving Fort Erie the train made stops at Stevensville, Welland Junction, and Marshville before entering Haldimand County

with stations at Moulton, Atterville, Darling Road, Canfield, Deans Station and Hagersville. The first train ran in 1873 to the delight of the southern peninsula.

In 1875 the Canada Southern bought the Erie & Niagara extending its reach into the northern peninsula. It was absorbed by the Michigan Central in 1894. Railroads have been a colourful part of our history and the ghosts of the steam locomotives still echo across the Niagara Peninsula.

AUTHOR'S NOTE: For a more complete treatment of the railways in Niagara see "Railways in the Niagara Peninsula" by John N. Jackson and John Burtniak, Mika Publishing Company, Belleville, Ontario, 1978. The book is available at your local public library.

STEAMSHIPS & SAILERS

With all the talk of roads and steam engines we must acknowledge that Niagara has been undeniably linked with ships for over two hundred years. We have already seen the impacted of canoes and sailers on the fur trade that opened up the west and gave the Niagara Peninsula its early importance. Between 1759, when the British captured Fort Niagara, and the 1780s when Butler's Rangers settled the west bank of the Niagara, water was the only means of communication available. Except for the few months when the lakes and rivers were frozen everything moved by canoe, boat or

In 1678 the French built three ships at Fort Frontenac (Kingston) to sail Lake Ontario securing the trade route to Niagara. They were the 10 ton "Frontenac", the "Le Generale" also of 10 tons and the 20 ton "Cataraqui". They and others built at Point au Baril and Fort Niagara carried troops and supplies to the various outposts on Lake Ontario until the fall of Quebec in 1760.

The first sailing ship to ply the upper waters of the Niagara was the 60 ton Brigantine, the "Griffon" launched from a creek on the

upper Niagara in 1679. It sailed up the river and crossed Lake Erie in just three days anchoring in the mouth of the Detroit River to gather supplies. She was lost on her return voyage from Green Bay, Wisconsin in that year.

When the British took possession of Fort Niagara business continued as usual, but all on the east bank of the river. With the exception of a small post at Fort Erie the peninsula was quiet.

With the outbreak of the American Revolution the British increased their presents on the lakes organizing the Provincial Marine under the British Army's Quartermaster General. It ran over fifty armed and unarmed vessels of every description; Schooners, luggers, brigs, snows, sloops and a lateen. It patrolled the lakes, acted as courier and transported military supplies and personnel to the various theatres of war. Despite their numbers they were hard pressed to keep up with the demands of outposts like Fort Niagara opening up the opportunity for settlement of the peninsula in 1781.

The beginning of economic growth of the Niagara Peninsula came with the opening of the Portage Road in 1790. Ships made their regular run from York to Queenston to off load cargo destined for the west. One traveler, J.C. Ogden, wrote in 1799: "At the lower landing, Queenston, the vessels discharge their cargoes, and take on furs brought from 300 to 1500 miles back. I have seen four vessels of 60 to 100 tons unloading at once and 60 wagons loaded in a day for the Upper Landing at Chippawa."

The most dramatic growth of the Peninsula took place with the opening of the Welland Canal in 1829. When the Annie & Jane nosed her way into Lock 1 at Port Dalhousie that chilly November day she changed forever the history of Niagara. Shipping became both the impetus and catalyst for industrial growth across the peninsula.

The opening of the canal slowly changed the design of the ships that plied the great lakes. The flared bows and wide transoms of the graceful lake schooners soon gave way to a less pleasing but more practical shape to take advantage of the canal. Canalers, as they were called, were more box like with flat bows and sterns with vertical sides to easily fit into the locks.

The canal also led to a thriving shipbuilding industry in Niagara. Besides the yards along the canal like Shickluna's and John P. Abbey's at Port Robinson, a shipbuilding company opened at Chippawa. The Niagara Harbour and Dock Company built the "Emerald" for James Macklem in 1844. Its run was Chippawa to Buffalo and Port Robinson carrying passengers and cargo.

The most luxurious steamship on the upper lakes was built at Chippawa in 1847. The "Canada" boasted an upper cabin that was 54.8 metres long and decorated with oil paintings of scenes of Canadian shore lines from Quebec to the Northwest. It included Brock's Monument and Navy Island. It had forty-two staterooms to accommodate its passengers in complete comfort. However, the career of the Canada was short lived. It ran aground near Detroit and her engines were removed in the winter of 1849-50.

In 1853 the famous St. Catharines shipbuilder, Louis Shickluna, built the "Clifton" at the Chippawa yard for Oliver Macklem to replace the "Emerald", however, with the decline in passenger traffic between Chippawa and Buffalo she was switched to the ferry service from Buffalo to Fort Erie. In 1860 she resumed the Niagara River run docking at both Chippawa and Fort Schlosser on the American side.

On the lower river steamboats became an important part of the fledgling tourist industry at Niagara Falls. In 1853 the much traveled Louis Shickluna oversaw the building of the "Zimmerman" at Niagara Dockyards for service on the Niagara-Toronto run. Oliver Macklem, the owner, named her for Samuel Zimmerman who had a financial interest in the Erie & Ontario Rail Road with which the "Zimmerman" connected at Niagara. The

"Zimmerman" went out of service in 1858 with the advent of the steam railways. She burned at her dock at Niagara in 1863. However, her engines were salvaged and put into the "City of Toronto".

In 1878 the Niagara Navigation Company renewed regular steamship passenger service from Queenston to Toronto. The Chicora was their first boat and they added a second in 1887 called the Cibola. The Chicora was in service for thirty-six years until she was retired and scrapped in 1914. The Cibola burned in the Niagara River in June of 1895.

In May of 1893 the Chippewa was launched and made the Lake Ontario run for forty-six years before being scrapped in 1939. The Hamilton Steamboat Company entered competition for the passenger service between Toronto and Queenston-Lewiston about 1905 with the steam turbine driven Turbinia. The Niagara Navigation Company countered with the Cayuga in 1907 and competition was fierce. In 1907 the Cayuga beat the Turbinia in an unofficial race, however, Turbinia's sister ship the Northumberland won the return engagement.

The Turbinia and Northumberland could not compete with the Cayuga and her sisters and they returned to the Toronto-Hamilton run after only two months. The Cayuga was the last of the lake steamers leaving service first in 1952 and after a revival in 1954 she retired for good in 1957. She was scrapped in 1961.

To this day water transportation remains an intricate part of the Niagara Story.

HISTORICAL NOTE: The more obscure types of ships operated by the Provincial Marine bear some explaining: Lugger: a vessel carrying a four cornered lugsail; Snow: a small sailing vessel carrying a main and fore mast and a supplementary trysail mast close behind the main mast; Lateen: a small sailing vessel having a single triangular sail.

CHAPTER THREE

COMMERCE OF SHAME

The history of Niagara has been shaped by many different ethnic groups since it was first settled in the 1780s. We begin with the experience of the blacks who came to Niagara as both slaves and freemen. However, before we look at the black experience in Niagara it is important that we look at the history of the slave trade that brought them to North America in the first place.

The African slave trade can be traced back to 1441 when the Portuguese raided the coast of Senegal returning to Portugal with black slaves. In 1445 six Portuguese ships went slaving on the African coast. They took mostly women and children as they could not catch the men. At first Spain resisted the temptation to import black slaves into its American colonies, but the demands of the planters soon won out. In 1517 the Spanish king gave permission for a limited number of African slaves to be brought to the new world. With an increasing demand black slaves soon flowed freely to the Spanish Main.

Slaves were not the first choice to work the fields. An adviser to the Swedish African Company said, "Slaves cost much, work reluctantly, require nothing from mechanics (tradesmen) as they go almost without clothes, and through ill treatment soon die; whereas the people from different parts of Europe, being free, intelligent and industrious, having wives and children, require all kinds of merchandise and mechanics, which would increase commerce." The problem was that few free whites could be lured to the plantations and those that did go out under contract rarely stayed beyond the first term.

It was almost impossible to stay out of the slave trade. The indigenous peoples of the Americas were unsuited to the rigors of work in the fields and died in great numbers, sometimes as many as twenty-five percent per year. African blacks on the other hand seemed to stand up well to the climate and the labours of sugar cane production. Suitable blacks were available in West Africa to be transported across the Atlantic.

The entry into the Atlantic Slave Trade by Great Britain can be traced to one event: that being the first slaving voyage of John Hawkins of Plymouth in 1562. The capital and ships were available in England to take advantage of what was seen as another profitable enterprise to be engaged in. Hawkins happened to be the first to realize the potential.

Hawkins arrived on the West African coast in December of 1562. He took on a cargo of pepper, ivory and four hundred slaves for Hispanola where the Spanish officials turned a blind eye to this intruder, so short of labour were the plantations.

He sailed again in 1564 under the backing of Queen Elizabeth I taking a town by force to do business. His third voyage in 1567 saw him transport five hundred black slaves. He was waylaid by the Spanish authorities this time, but British involvement in the slave trade was firmly established.

Because of the prevailing winds and currents the slavers first landfall in the new world was the Caribbean. The major slave ports thus began there. Bridgetown (Barbados), Basseterre (St. Kitts), St. John (Antigua) and Kingston (Jamaica) became the focal points of the slave trade in the islands. Charleston, South Carolina became the most prominent port in the American Colonies. The quality of slaves reaching the Carolinas was poor as the Caribbean ports

took the best as the ships passed through. After 1750 direct trade with the African coast became the norm in North America.

Aside from the early beginnings of the trade, when blacks were gathered in raids on the native villages, slaves were obtained by trading with the local rulers for captives taken in the constant wars that plagued the area. In times of peace the local king would also sell some of his own people to gain the profits from the trade. The traders built forts and factories along the west coast of Africa as well as trading at the established cities. Cities such as Benin, which thrived long before contact with Europeans, became centres of the trade.

Once aboard ship the infamous "middle passage" had to be endured by the prisoners. At best the slaves were crammed into the hold of a ship with barely room to move. The slaver would feed them food that they were used to and allow them to exercise on deck when conditions permitted. At worse they would spend the five week voyage sealed up in the hold with poor food and no exercise.

Many died of disease or committed suicide rather than endure the horror that was visited upon them.

Once landed in Charleston or some other port they were forced to submit to the auction. After the humiliation of being stripped naked and being examined by prospective buyers they were sold to the highest bidder. Slaves were sold without regard to Family units and many a mother wept bitterly as her husband and children were shipped off in different directions never to be seen again.

The southern colonies were not the only ones to have slaves. New England and the middle colonies also participated in the trade. The Dutch had African slaves in New Amsterdam as early as 1628. When the English gained control of New Amsterdam in 1664 it renamed the colony New York. Soon slaves laws were passed similar to the laws in other colonies. In 1684 a law was passed recognizing slavery as an institution in New York.

Slavery never became a permanent institution in Pennsylvania. Although William

Penn, the colonies founder, believed in slavery most other Quakers felt that slavery was wrong. The Mennonites issued a resolution in 1688 that stated: "Now, although they are black, we cannot conceive . . . to have them as slaves. . . . There is a saying, that we should do to all men like as we will be done ourselves; making no difference of what generation, descent, or colour they are."

With the outbreak of the American Revolution the stage was set for the introduction of slavery into the Niagara Peninsula.

TOWARD EMANCIPATION

The Treaty of Paris affirmed British control of French possession in North America with the exception of the Islands of St. Pierre and Miquelon. Although French Canadians did own some black slaves, slavery never really took hold in New France. The lack of demand for cheap labour was the chief reason for it.

The British allowed the French to retain their slaves and this was reaffirmed by the Treaty of Paris. In 1774 the boundaries of Quebec were extended to the Ohio River leaving the slave population of all of Canada at just under one hundred.

General James Murray, the commander at Quebec, sought to change the attitudes in the new reorganized colony. He encouraged the importation of slaves and wrote to a friend in New York in November of 1763 asking for "two stout young fellows" and- that they should have "a communication with the ladys (sic)" and be happy- "for each a clean young wife." While these four black slaves were to be his, he saw broader possibilities: "Black slaves are certainly the only people to be depended upon, but . . . they should be born in one or other of our northern colonies, as the winters here will not agree with a native of the torrid zone."

With the outbreak of the American Revolution in 1776 the position of black slaves changed dramatically. The British, seeing slavery as a major weakness of the southern colonies offered emancipation to all slaves who volunteered to serve with their forces. There was a thin line between blacks who surrendered to British officers and those captured as spoils of war. Those captured were sold and many loyalist regiments were involved including Butler's Rangers. One raid on Balliston, New York yielded seven or more slaves who were thus sold as spoils of war. Captain John Monroe, who commanded the raid, later declared, "he never considered these captured Negroes as ordinary prisoners of war and consequently did not report to the Commander-in-Chief or any other Commanding Officer," for selling Negroes was "customary." It is impossible to know how many slaves entered Canada during that period.

Late in the war Sir Guy Carleton, Commander-in-Chief of all British forces in North America, guaranteed that all slaves would be free who, upon seeking refuge behind British lines, made formal claim to British protection. At war's end George Washington insisted that all slaves be returned to their owners in compliance with the Provisional Articles of November 1782, which stated in part: "His Britannic Majesty shall with all convenient speed, and without causing any destruction, or carrying away any Negroes, or other property of the American Inhabitants, withdraw all his Armies." Carleton stuck to his guns however and finally agreed to compensate owners rather than go back on the proclamations made during the war. Thus many free blacks were evacuated to British territory during 1783. Most freed blacks who came north ended up in Nova Scotia. Most Blacks who came to Quebec came as slaves owned by United Empire Loyalists.

Among the prominent loyalists who brought slaves with them to Quebec west of the Ottawa River were Richard Cartwright, Peter Russell and William Jarvis. Joseph Brant, Chief of the Six Nations settlement at

Brantford kept slaves on his estate. Although small in number, slaves continued to be bought and sold in Quebec into the early 1790s.

The situation was to take a dramatic turn with the arrival of John Graves Simcoe who became the first Lieutenant Governor of the newly created Province of Upper Canada. He had, as a member of parliament in 1790, condemned slavery, writing privately that it was opposed by both Christianity and the British Constitution. He said that he would not give assent to any law that "discriminates by dishonest policy between the natives of Africa, America or Europe."

Upon arriving at Niagara in 1792 he spoke of issuing a proclamation freeing all slaves. He welcomed black settlers but refused to allow them to take up land in segregated communities opting instead for a policy of integration. Through all this Simcoe's chief aim was to abolish slavery altogether.

In March of 1793 Simcoe questioned the legality of slavery while declaring it a danger to the new province. On March 21 Peter Mar-

tin, a Negro employed by Colonel John Butler, appeared before the Executive Council made up of Simcoe, Chief Justice William Osgoode and Peter Russell, owner of many slaves, and told them how a Negro girl named Chloe Cooley, who belonged to William Vrooman of Queenston, was bound and, despite violent resistance by her, was spirited across the Niagara River and sold to Americans. Furthermore a witness testified that many slave owners were going to do the same in anticipation of a declaration of emancipation.

Simcoe moved quickly. Attorney General John White introduced a bill in the Legislative Assembly to gradually abolish slavery. It was a compromise that allowed all sides, abolitionist and slave holder to save face, however the slave owners were not happy.

The act did not free a single slave but set the wheels in motion for the eventual elimination of slavery. It allowed for slaves then in the province to remain in bondage for life and no slaves could be imported into the province. Any children born into slavery were to be freed on their twenty-fifth birthday and any children born to them before they reached the age of twenty-five were free at birth.

The act was unpopular among slave owners and John White was unseated at the next election. When Simcoe left Upper Canada an attempt was made to undo what he had accomplished. In 1798 a loyalist from Virginia, Christopher Robinson, member for Addington and Ontario, introduced a bill to allow immigrants to bring Negro slaves into the province. The bill passed by a vote of eight to four, however, Robert Hamilton of Queenston and Richard Cartwright bottled the bill up in the upper chamber until the session ended. The chief opposition to slavery came from an unlikely source. The Solicitor General, Robert Isaac Dey Gray, a slave owner himself, blocked any attempt to subvert Simcoe's work.

Despite the law some slaves continued to come into the province. As late as 1809 John Thomas of Brant County brought slaves in from Tennessee. On August 28, 1833 the British parliament passed an act outlawing slavery in all the British American colonies thus completing what Simcoe had started forty years previously. The stage was set for the Underground Railroad.

THE UNDERGROUND RAILROAD

In the same year that the Assembly of Upper Canada passed the law that would eventually eliminate slavery the Congress of the United States was passing the first Fugitive Slave Act. The law forbad any person from keeping or helping an escaped slave. To this point any slave who reached the north was free. Even free blacks became fearful as unscrupulous policemen would pick up anyone for the reward. It only took another white man to swear ownership of a Black to have him or her sold to someone in a slave state.

Word slowly spread that Upper Canada meant freedom without fear of recapture. The migration of blacks began as a trickle and before it was over became a torrent. Most settled in areas close to the border because of the lack of funds and the desire to eventually return to their former homes to seek out families that were left behind. In Niagara they settled at the Twelve Mile Creek as well as the area around Newark in the northern peninsula.

Most slaves who attempted to escape to the north were from the border slave states such as Tennessee and Maryland. They often chose a Saturday night to make their getaway as Sunday was the one day they were off and would not be missed. It took a particularly inventive and courageous man or woman to attempt escape. The probability of recapture was high and slave catchers were relentless in their pursuit. They would head out and cover as much ground as they could that first night. After that they hid by day and traveled by night until they reached a place in the north where help could be found. Despite the Fugitive Slave Act upwards of 10,000 slaves found freedom in the northern states. By 1815, aided by abolitionists in the north, who were mainly Quakers, an estimated one thousand slaves found freedom in Upper Canada.

In the era before and just after the War of 1812 Blacks were accepted both officially and by their neighbours. They served in the militia and were integrated with white troops receiving modest promotions with their white counterparts. At the outbreak of the War of 1812 the position of the fugitive slave became rather precarious. If the Americans managed to drive the British from Upper Canada and secure it for themselves there was no doubt but the Fugitive Slave Act would be vigorously applied. Richard Pierpont, an escaped slave living at Newark petitioned to raise a company of Blacks to fight in the Lincoln Militia. As a result Captain

Robert Runchey, a white officer, commanded this Company of Coloured Men.

Runchey's company arrived at Queenston Heights as part of Sheaffe's reinforcements and saw action there. Twenty-seven members of the company fought along side the Glengarry Light Infantry in an attempt to repel the Americans at Fort George in May of 1813. They supplied part of the garrison at Burlington and Fort Mississauga until late in 1813 when most of the battalion companies of the Lincoln Militia were used as labour, building fortifications, acting as teamsters and foraging for supplies.

The tempo of fugitives coming to Upper Canada picked up after the war. Blacks, both slave and free were encouraged to immigrate. Sir John Colborne, Lieutenant Governor of Upper Canada answered an inquiry from free Blacks in Cincinnati, Ohio as to the possibility of their coming to the province this way: "Tell the Republicans on your side of the line that we do not know men by their colour, If you come to us you will be entitled to all the privileges of the rest of his Majesty's sub-

jects."

The stricter Fugitive Slave Act passed by the U.S. Congress in 1850 opened the flood gates and the "Underground Railway" began in earnest. The system, although informal, adopted railroad terms in describing itself. People who hid the fugitives in their homes were called "agents"; destination points were "stations" and those that transported them were called "conductors."

The most famous conductor on the underground railroad was Harriet Tubman. A fugitive slave who had escaped from her master in 1849, she made nineteen trips into the United States, at great risk to herself, to bring slaves to freedom.

Harriet Tubman made her first trip in 1851 bringing eleven fugitives to St. Catharines. She settled in St. Catharines opening a boarding house for fugitive slaves on North Street behind the British Methodist Episcopal Church. She was so successful that the slave owners put a price on her head of $40,000 dead or alive.

For fugitive slaves freedom was not assured until they actually reached British territory. Capture by vigilant marshalls or slave catchers was possible even in sight of the prize. They would hide until dark and then, with the help of abolitionists both black and white, slip across the swift flowing Niagara River to safety.

The young black man gave a start as the door to attic swung open. He was prepared to run regardless of the consequences rather than go back to his owner in Virginia. It turned out to be Harriet Tubman, their conductor. He had heard the many stories about her told in whispers in the slave quarters of the plantation and he had always discounted most of them as being to fantastic. Now he knew the truth of those stories. He remembered that night when he was about to fall asleep and that lilting song had slipped into the slave quarters: "When that old chariot comes, who's going with me?" Without thinking he heard himself sing back, "When that old chariot comes, I'm going with you!"

After slipping out she had led them through woods and swamps. She had pleaded, coerced and threatened to get them this far. One man was so frightened on that first night that he wanted to go back. To his dismay she had pulled a gun from her pack and told him to "move or die."

They said that they was in Black Rock, New York. Now they made their way to the river's edge where a long boat waited. A white man came out of the gloom making him step back in alarm, a soothing voice reassured him and he climbed into the boat with his bundle on his shoulder. The boat shoved off and even in the darkness he could tell that the river was fast moving. The two oarsmen leaned back on their oars propelling the craft toward the opposite shore. Suddenly the oars were tossed and he could hear voices as someone guided their boat into the bank.

As he landed he glanced furtively over his shoulder expecting to see a slave catcher flicking his whip against his riding boot. A voice out of the darkness said, "It's OK!, this here is Canada."

CHAPTER FOUR

THE SMITHY

In the early 1820s the peninsula was still struggling to reestablish the industries decimated during the war. A deep recession that followed the conflict slowed the process greatly as we have seen in the problems encountered by Merritt.

On the sight of the Battle of Lundy's Lane a small community began to grow. Austin Morse was a furniture maker and undertaker whose chapel still operates on Main Street in Niagara Falls today. Andrew Moss made cabinets, James Skinner was a harness maker, John Misener ran a wagon building operation and William Gurnan was the indispensable blacksmith.

One of the more prolific endeavors of those days was the distillery. One such operation was located at the foot of Murray Street in, what is now, Queen Victoria Park. It was a stone structure and was there to take advantage of the spring that ran down the ravine. It was abandoned in 1826 and eventually housed Barnett's Museum.

St. Johns, near Fonthill, was one community that had escaped damage during the war and prospered. It boasted many mills and a number of distilleries. An iron foundry, tannery, saddle maker, a woolen factory and many others rounded out this thriving town. The Welland Canal put St. Johns into decline as industry moved closer to the canal banks and today little remains of its former glory.

In the southern part of the peninsula the Sugar Loaf sported a community that included saw mills and grist mills. It also had a blacksmith, harness maker, furniture maker and the inevitable distillery.

One of the most important workman in the community was the blacksmith. The first thing the pioneers demanded upon arriving in

the peninsula in 1781 was the services of a good smithy. We always associate the blacksmith with shoeing horses, but his business went far beyond that. He made everything from door hinges to wagon wheels.

The blacksmith shop was a miniature factory. The heart of the shop was the forge that was made of brick. It was set on a stone foundation with a square brick chimney that went up through the roof to a height of four feet above the ridge pole. The hearth was a square box twelve inches deep set next to the chimney. The bottom of the hearth was a slab of iron with a hole in the centre to take the air nozzle or tuyere as it was called. The tuyere was a hollow, slotted iron bulb attached to a pipe leading to the bellows. Air could be directed to one side of the hearth or the other by the use of an iron rod that rotated it. The brick work was extended to form a table on which the smithy could organize his work or leave finished pieces to cool.

The bellows was a huge leather lung eight feet long and four feet across that was mounted behind the chimney. A large stone was placed on the top so as to create a constant pressure allowing a gentle stream of air to keep the coals hot. If the smithy needed a little extra heat he pulled vigorously on the wooden handle that was attached to a chain and extended to the front of the forge.

If the forge was the heart of the shop then the anvil was the soul. It was a two hundred and fifty pound block of iron that measured five inches across, twenty inches long and had a sixteen inch horn curving out from one end. Its top was a slab of steel welded to the wrought iron base. Two holes were cut in the rear part of heel of the anvil. The hardy hole was square to fit the many forging tools used

by the smithy. The pritchel hole was three-eighths of an inch and round. It was used for punching jobs such as knocking nails out of old horseshoes.

The placement of the anvil was very important. Because the iron had to be heated at least once, if not more, the anvil had to be close to the fire. It was usually placed with the horn facing the fire. The height of the anvil was also critical. The blacksmith custom fitted his anvil to match his needs. If it was too high he would wear himself out swinging his hammer; if too low his hammer would not strike the iron squarely. Ideally, the bottom of the smithy's natural hammer swing matched the height of the anvil.

The setting of the anvil was an exact science, for once in place it could not be moved. It was mounted on the top of a post that was sunk four or five feet in the ground. With his anvil in place and coals glowing red in the hearth, the blacksmith was ready to do his work.

The iron that the smithy worked with came from a bloomery furnace and showed a crystal structure. After forging the crystals formed a grain that allowed the iron to bend without breaking.

The Blacksmith often had to draw the iron to make it thinner and wider. Heating the iron until it was red hot he then swung it to the anvil and struck it with his set hammer until it was no longer pliable enough to work. He would repeat the heating operation until he was satisfied that he had a workable piece of material.

The blacksmith was an important part of the early communities of Niagara. Without him the progress we have seen would not have been possible.

CHAPTER FIVE

SURVIVAL ON THE FRONTIER

Life was hard for the ordinary farmers struggling to survive in the early 19th century. Many lived in isolation along the creeks that flowed into the Niagara from Willoughby and Bertie townships or into the Welland River from Wainfleet, Crowland and Humberstone. Rebuilding houses and barns drained what little capital they had. Most made due with the crude dwellings that had all but disappeared as prosperity had come to the peninsula at the turn of the century.

The struggle to survive held the undivided attention of the entire family. Chores were completed before all else. As soon as a child was old enough to comprehend he or she was given a task, simple at first, but they picked up their share of the burden as they grew.

For us, who simply flick a switch when we want light or run down to the super market for our meat and groceries, it is hard to imagine having to plan carefully months in advance to light, heat and feed a household, but that is exactly what the pioneers had to do. One eye had to be kept on the wood pile. Was there enough to last the winter? Is it time to cut next year's supply? If the farmer miscalculated he would have to burn green wood with the resultant smoke that inevitably would linger in the room regardless of how well the chimney was drawing.

The laying up of preserves for the winter was a necessary task for every pioneer housewife. The fall butchering and the preservation of meat was calculated to see the family through as well as to provide income from the sale of pork and beef to the military garrisons and the growing towns.

All the cooking and heating in the pioneer house emanated from the big fireplace in the kitchen. The fire was kept blazing during the day in fall and winter as the door was often left open, despite the cold, for light and to clear smoke from the house.

For cooking purposes the fireplace was outfitted with an iron crane with hooks to hold pots. By swinging the crane out the meal could be checked without leaning over the fire. Baking was done either in a small stove fitted into the fireplace or in a crude oven built in the yard. Winter and summer the bread was baked in this manner: wood was piled into the oven and burned, effectively preheat the oven. The ashes were scraped out and the bread inserted, cooking with the heat retained in the walls of the oven.

The utensils used in the kitchen were crude by our standards. They were often hand made from wood. Spoons, ladles and forks were laboriously carved by the man of the house. Bread pans for raising the dough were hollowed out of solid pieces of wood. The large, long handled wooden paddle used for putting the bread in and out of the outdoor oven was often cut from a single piece as well.

Health was another problem that plague our forbearers in the 1820s. Fifty-five percent of the children did not live to age five. Doctors were often military surgeons located at the various forts around the peninsula. Doctors began to appear in the larger centres like Niagara and St. Catharines but were too far away to be of use to most of the isolated farms and communities.

With the shortage of trained medical doctors it fell to the more educated in the neighbourhood to fill the gap. These "folk" doctors, who were usually women, kept a supply of bandages and medicines obtained from the

military surgeons on hand to treat their patients. They were often versed in the home remedies brought from Europe as well as those of the local Indians. These same women also acted as midwives and were sent for when the time for delivery of a baby was near.

Chronic diarrhea, dysentery and cholera, caused by the primitive sanitation, were the chief health problems threatening the populace. The local home remedy might be the only medicine available. For the above mentioned ailments this would include Oak bark. The practitioner boiled an ounce of the inner bark in a pint of water and administer it to the patient. Acorns and Blackberry root were also used with good results.

Children were in constant danger from diseases that are considered little more than inconveniences today. Measles and chicken pox were dangerous. Many children died of fevers brought on by teething.

Another danger facing the pioneer was the possibility of injury. Serious wounds re-

sulting from chopping wood were fairly common. The treatment was to apply a court plaster, bind the wound tightly and hope for the best. A court plaster was made with isinglass, a gelatin concocted from the air bladders of fresh water fish and silk. Anxious watch was kept for any sign of infection that almost always led to amputation of the offending limb. Before the age of anesthetics such operations were painful as well as dangerous.

The patient was taken to the nearest surgeon, usually Ft. George or Ft. Erie. Liberal doses of rum or some other alcohol were administered to dull the senses. Knives and saws were warmed up to lessen the shock and the doctor went to work. If the person were lucky they fainted at the first touch, sparing them the ordeal that the cutting and sawing would entail.

The people of the peninsula struggled for a better life for their families in the wilderness frontier that was Niagara.

CHAPTER SIX
THE HARVEST

The most critical time of the fall for the farmer was the harvest. On this hinged his livelihood and the survival of his family. Would an early frost damage the crop? Would the rains hold off until the fields were cleared? All these things plagued the pioneer as he waited for his crop to ripen.

In preparation for the harvest the equipment had to be inspected and repaired where necessary. Sickles and scythes were sharpened and flails made ready. Sweeping the barn floor to prepare it for threshing was a job for which the children took responsibility.

With one eye on the weather the farmer walked his fields checking the grain to satisfy himself that it was ready for harvesting. If he didn't have children old enough to help with the cutting and gathering he would hire some farm labourers from the nearest town or if the weather was holding neighbours gathered and helped each other bring in the crops.

Haggai Skinner looked over the flowing field of wheat that was about to be cut. He let his mind wander over all that he'd been through in the last seven years. He had been working this very field in 1813 when the American patrol had snatched him up and made him a prisoner-of-war. It angered him still when he thought it. At sixty-four he was exempt from militia service, yet they had taken him anyway. For almost a year he had languished in prison to be repatriated in July, 1814 in time to hear of the bloody battle at Lundy's Lane. He arrived home to find the family in mourning for Timothy Skinner who was killed at the Battle of Chippawa earlier in the month. He was buried somewhere on the battlefield. The American refusal to allow the recovery of the dead after the battle was something else that rankled Haggai. He had

gone to the battle sight after the harvest that year in a vain hope of finding a clue to the burial spot, but found nothing.

He was roused from his musings by the impatient stamping of the horses who seemed anxious to get started. Seeing the boys ready to gather the cuttings into sheaves he began to swing his sickle in a smooth, rhythmic stroke developed over sixty years of farming.

As the grain was cut the workers following behind gathered them up into sheaves and loaded them on the wagon for transport back to the barn. The work day began at first light and except for meals went straight through until sundown. Often lunch was brought to the fields so as to loss as little time as possible.

Once cut the grain was moved to the barn for flailing. The flail was made up of two sticks each about three feet long. A leather strap or a piece of rope joined these together. The grain was laid out on the floor and the men began beating the stalks to separate the grain. Once this was completed the stalks were gathered, shaken and discarded.

The grain was swept into a broad wooden shovel with a handle on either side. In a process called winnowing the grain was tossed in the air allowing the chaff to blow away while the heavier grain fell back into the shovel. We can imagine the field day that the farm poultry had snatching up the grain that invariably fell to the ground. The grain was then bagged for the trip to the mill.

Wheat most often went to the mill to be ground into flour. Oats and barley were usually sold for feed or, in the case of barley, to be made into beer or liquor by one of the local brewers or distillers.

1. Cutting crops with scythes...
2. Gathering sheaves
3. Grain harvest moved into barns ready for threshing...
4. Flails separate grain from stalks
5. Raw grain taken to local mill...
- water-powered grist mills ground flour

Transportation to the market was a thorny problem in the 1820s. In Humberstone and Wainfleet the mills at the Sugar Loaf had to be reached over swampy terrain. In Stamford the Bridgewater Mills, burned by the Americans in 1814, had not been rebuilt making the long trek to either the mills in Thorold or to the Short Hills.

If heavy rain fell the roads became impassable and often the crop had to be moved in other ways. Those on a waterway sometimes tried to float the grain to the mill, however, this often led to a soaking leaving the grain useless for milling.

The mills in the Niagara Peninsula were water powered. The grain was poured into a hopper and was grounded between two large stones. The flour dropped through a meal trough and was packed in barrels for storage and shipment. Payment for the milling was often made by giving the miller a share of the grain. The miller also would act as the farmer's agent in the sale of the ground grain as well.

In order to produce an adequate grade of flour the mill stones had to be sharp. It was necessary from time to time to deepen the furrows in the wheel and to dress the surface. A crane was used to lift and turn over the upper stone. The furrows were then deepened with steel picks to bring them up to specification. To test the levels of the stone a wooden bar with its edge smeared with red clay was drawn across the surface. The high parts with red clay smeared on them were then dressed off until the surface was level.

The next problem facing the millers and merchants of the peninsula was moving the flour to market. Produce from Humberstone and Wainfleet moved by water down the Welland River to Chippawa and then along the Portage Road to the busy port of Queenston. Grain from Thorold, Grantham and Stamford moved by wagon to Queenston. From here freight of every type was loaded on sailing vessels for York, Montreal and Quebec City.

HISTORICAL NOTE: Haggai Skinner's farm was located in Stamford Township in the vicinity of present day Mcleod Road and Drummond Road.

CHAPTER SEVEN

PREPARING FOR WINTER

As the crops ripened in the fields in the fall of 1820 and harvest time drew near preparations began for the coming winter. Chores essential for the survival of the family in the harsh days to come filled their waking hours. Some of the older children inspected the mortar that sealed up the cracks in the log wall of the house. Any weaknesses that the cold winds of winter might explore were repaired.

There were winter clothes to make as well as preserves of wild berries and garden vegetables to be put up. At this time of the year the women headed for the nearest marsh to pick the Elderberries and blueberries that were abundant there. In the Welland area the Wainfleet Marsh was a popular spot for berry picking.

The butchering bee was a social occasion as well as a working day. Several neighbours gathered in turn at each other's farms to slaughter and dress the meat for the smoke house. Beef was by far the favourite, however, more often than not it was hogs that provided the larder with most of its stock.

Before the killing of the hogs began a large kettle was set in the yard and a fire built under it. Usually one of the older boys was given the task of keeping the fire going to insure that the water was kept boiling. After being killed the carcass was scolded in the kettle to facilitate the removal of the pigs body hair. The fat was then gathered, cleaned, melted down and set in containers to cool. This became lard and would show up in the cakes and pie crusts that winter.

Smoking was the way that meat was preserved. Shoulders and sides of beef and pork were hung in the small building usually situated near the house. Sticks of birch, hickory or maple smoldered filling the place with smoke thus curing the meat. Sometimes corn cobs were used instead of wood. After being smoked the meat was covered with cotton cloth and given a coat of whitewash to discourage spoilage. The smoke house often doubled as a storage area for the cured meat.

Cuts of meat unsuitable for smoking were ground up and made into sausage. Preparing the intestines of the slaughtered pigs the women spent the day stuffing the gut with pork and beef flavoured with salt and any other herbs that could be obtained either from the surrounding land or purchased in town. The head and feet were soaked and scraped, then boiled, the former to make head cheese, the latter souse. As you can see little of the animal was wasted by the early pioneers.

After completing the butchering the tallow from the slaughter was used to make candles and soap. The shortage of hard currency made the purchase of these two commodities out of the reach of most farmers. However, they often had to buy extra tallow to ensure a supply of candles to last the season.

Candle making was quite an art in itself. The large kettle in the yard that was used in the butchering was half filled with water that was kept hot with a small fire. The tallow was placed in the kettle and allowed to melt. Six cotton wicks, each ten to twelve inches long were tied to sticks two feet long. Holding two sticks in her right hand the woman of the house began dipping the wicks through the floating tallow allowing them to pick up a little with each pass until they reached the desired thickness. The sticks were then hung between two forked sticks to allow the candles to harden and the process began all over again.

It took experience to make a smooth can-

dle that burned evenly. There was nothing worse than trying to read or sew by the light of a sputtering, smoking candle. A good candle maker got a yield of a dozen candles to the pound and could process ten pound of tallow at a sitting.

One of the sources of ready cash to the farmers of the peninsula was potash. This product was in great demand and lead to the deforestation of much of the peninsula. Potash was made by cutting down trees and allowing the leaves and twigs to dry. They were then stacked and burned until the whole was reduced to ashes. Carefully raking the ashes off the top of the pile, the farmer poured them into a container, called a "leach", with lime and water. The lye produced by this mixture was drained through the bottom of the "leach" into an iron pot. The lye was then boiled until it thickened and was poured into a kettle shaped half cooler. The final produce was a very hard, brown material that was packed two to a standard oak barrel. Each barrel weighted about seven hundred

pounds and would fetch the farmer $40.

The hard working people of the peninsula had little time for relaxation and fun. Much of the time they would combine leisure activities with the necessities of survival. An hour or two of fishing rested the farmer and added variety to the family diet. A morning beside a known deer trail was both relaxing and added to the larder for the winter.

After the chores were done the family gathered and played checkers while mother sat in her rocking chair and sewed. Books were scarce especially after the war, however, reading was popular and whenever the opportunity arose it was worth the expenditure of a candle. Books were often passed from one family to the other in the district. The first library in the peninsula was set up in 1824 at Brown's Bridge located at the foot of Pelham Road in present day Welland.

With all this activity the farmer kept one eye on the weather and the other on his crop. The harvest was the most critical time for him and his family. Their survival depended on it.

CHAPTER EIGHT

RIPPLES, HECKLES & NIDDY-NODDIES

Industry flourished in the Niagara Peninsula of the 1850s. Factories sprang up in proximity to the Welland Canal producing myriad products from iron work to flour. One of the industries that began to see major changes was weaving. The canal and its resultant increase in water power made the building of woolen mills a practical enterprise. To this time their were few woolen mills operating and it was a cottage industry that supplemented the income of many farm families. Flax was the predominant source of spinning and weaving material. Since flax is used to make linen many fine examples of handiwork were evident in the pioneer home. Only in the early 1860s did sheep appear in the province in large numbers. Problems of wolves and the severe winters kept farmers from raising flocks of sheep. Advance technology and the disappearance of predators solved the problem giving rise to a flourishing wool industry.

Hannah moved among the small flax seedlings, plucking the weeds that were attempting to get a foothold in the field. The soft earth caressed her bare feet as she carefully places them between the thickly sown plants. The seedlings were hardy and when stepped upon sprang back with the resiliency of youth. They were sown close together so that they would grow straight and tall. As they grew in size they smothered the weeds providing they were kept down in the early stages of growth. Soon the backbreaking work would be unnecessary.

Hannah's family anxiously watched the flax crop for the first signs of small, blue flowers standing brightly against the green of the leaves and stems. Inspection showed that his would be a bumper crop.

Toward the end of July Hannah's husband, Peter, announced that the bottom of the stems were beginning to turn yellow, time for the harvest. The family began to get the flax off pulling the plants up by the roots so as to get as long a fibre as possible. Next it was tied in bundles and stood up in the fields to dry for a couple of days.

Once dry the bundles were stacked by the front porch where Peter had set his ripple, an iron instrument attached to a bench. The flax was drawn through the ripple's teeth to remove the seed, which was saved for next years planting.

The fibre used in the making of thread lay between the bark and the stem itself. The seedless flax next had to be retted, that is the rotting of the stem just enough to allow the fibres to be separated without damaging it. As with most of their neighbours this family used the dew retting method. The flax was spread thinly on the ground and was wetted by the dew and the rain. The sun dried the flax through the day and then the process was repeated over a two week period. It was turned frequently as too long an exposure weakened the fibres.

Hannah tied the dried out flax in bundles again to await breaking. This was a job for Peter as muscle was required for this extremely dirty work. The break consisted of several wooden bars mounted on a frame; and a wooden knife with several blunt blades, which was fitted between the bars. The knife was raised and the bundle of flax held across the bars. Peter brought the knife down sharply breaking the brittle straw but leaving the fibre undamaged. He then beat it with a scutching knife against a board until bark and stem fell away leaving the fibre alone.

carding the wool

flax Ripple

flax break

Reel

swift

typical ontario Loom

shuttle

Peter next turned to the heckle, a board with long, sharp steel teeth protruding from it. He drew the flax fibre through the teeth of a coarse heckle first and then graduated to a finer one. The heckle straightened the fibres and separated them. The coarser fibre, called tow, was saved for making rope. The heckled fibres were as soft as hair, ready for Hannah to arrange on the distaff for spinning into thread.

Hannah spent hours at her spinning wheel turning the jumble of flax fibre into delicate thread. Her's was a small Irish wheel driven by a foot treadle. The treadle revolved the spindle at a great speed and the thread was twisted, drawn in and wound on a bobbin. Her neighbour had a large walking wheel that was turned by hand, the spinner stepping back a few paces to draw out the thread.

The growth in the sheep population brought wool to the forefront. It was handled in a slightly different way then the flax. In the early summer, when the sheep no longer needed their heavy coat of wool, they were sheared and the women washed the fleece in warm water with homemade soap. The fleece was then spread out on a clean surface, usually grass, to dry.

The matted wool was then picked clean of any foreign matter such a twig and burrs, which separated it somewhat giving it an appearance of being soft and fluffy. The wool was carded next. Two rectangular pieces of wood covered with leather, with handles placed at right angles held bent wire teeth. A handful of wool was placed on one of the cards and held on the knee. The other card was drawn across its mate a number of times until the wool was combed evenly with the strands running in the same direction. By reversing the combing action the wool automatically formed a roll ready for spinning.

The wool was spun much as the flax was. When the wool was spun it was removed from the wheel onto a reel, which measured the yarn and arranged it in a skein, which was forty turns on the fifty-four foot reel. Another device that measured the yarn as it came off the spindle was the niddy-noddy. Grasping it in the centre with the left hand, the person swung and turned it to a song. At the end of the song there was forty rounds of yarn on the niddy-noddy.

With the advent of the big mills and the lower prices of imports, the cottage spinners slowly disappeared from the Peninsula. However, their skill and dedication will always be a part of our heritage.

CHAPTER NINE

THE POWER OF THE PEN

In this age of instant communication, with television, fax machines and the information super highway, we take for granted that a story that breaks at 5:30 will be common knowledge by 5:35. Our pioneer forefathers in the Niagara Peninsula, however, relied entirely on the printed word to hear the news of the day.

When John Graves Simcoe established the first capital of Upper Canada at Newark (Niagara-on-the-Lake) in 1792 he felt that a newspaper was essential. In June of 1793 the first edition of the "Upper Canada Gazette or American Oracle" came off the press. This was not really a newspaper in the true sense of the word because it carried little more than government announcements.

The first independent newspaper in Niagara was the Canadian Constitution published by the Tiffany brothers, Gideon and Sylvester. This paper soon folded. Sylvester started the Niagara Herald in 1801, which garnered a large readership across the peninsula. In 1807 Joseph Willcocks, who was to become the infamous turncoat of the War of 1812, began the Upper Canada Guardian. Willcocks used his paper to attack the government at every turn gaining a excellent reputation among the locals. His paper died with the outbreak of the war and his subsequent defection to the Americans. During the war a paper called The Bee appeared with James Durand as its editor, but the unsettled conditions force it out of business.

The end of the War of 1812 saw three newspapers spring from the ashes. The first was the St. Davids Spectator, edited by Robert Cockerel. The second was called the Niagara Spectator based in Newark and last was The Gleaner, also in Newark, published

by Samuel Heron.

The Gleaner prospered and over twenty years gained a reputation as one of the leading newspapers in Upper Canada. The St. Davids and the Niagara Spectator, however met tragic ends.

The St. Davids Spectator found itself on the wrong side of provincial politics in 1818. It carried a speech by James Durand, former editor of The Bee, and suffered from the backlash. The paper soon ceased publication.

The Niagara Spectator's editor Bartimus Ferguson printed a libelous letter from Robert Gourlay, a prominent agitator of the day, which attacked the Family Compact. All the weight the government could bring to bear fell on the Spectator.

Ferguson was fined 50 pounds and sentenced to eighteen months in jail. On appeal eleven months were knock off his sentence and Ferguson moved to Hamilton were he founded that city's first newspaper. Within a year that venture failed and Ferguson died soon after.

Perhaps the most famous newspaper to come out of Niagara was The Colonial Advocate. It stirred the pot of reform in Upper Canada as had no other paper in our history.

William Lyon Mackenzie; bookseller, publisher, parliamentarian and rebel; moved to Queenston in 1823. The politics of the day distressed him to no end and on arriving in Queenston he founded the Colonial Advocate to write in opposition to the Family Compact. This close knit group of families ruled Upper Canada through a system of patronage.

William Lyon Mackenzie looked over the latest edition of his new newspaper, The Colonial Advocate, with some satisfaction.

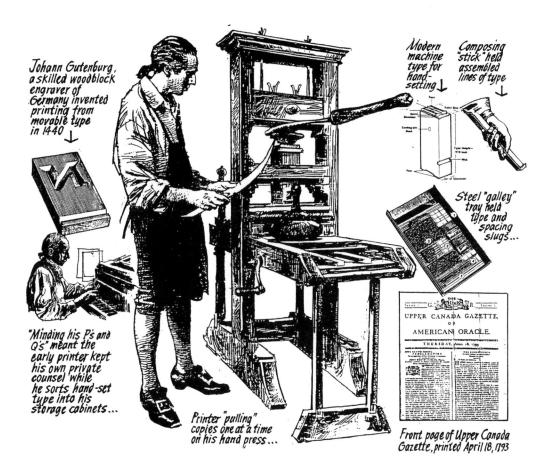

Johann Gutenburg, a skilled woodblock engraver of Germany invented printing from movable type in 1440 ↓

Modern machine type for hand-setting ↓

Composing "stick" held assembled lines of type ↓

Steel "galley" tray held type and spacing slugs...

"Minding his P's and Q's" meant the early printer kept his own private counsel while he sorts hand-set type into his storage cabinets...

Printer "pulling" copies one at a time on his hand press...

Front page of Upper Canada Gazette, printed April 18, 1793

The mast head never ceased to give him pleasure:

COLONIAL ADVOCATE

And Journal of Agriculture, Manufactures, and Commerce.

Published by W.L. Mackenzie, Bookseller, Queenston, Upper Canada. Thursday, June 3, 1824. Price 5d. (Vol. 1. No. 3.) Mackenzie began to read:

"John Beverly Robinson, Esquire, Attorney General of Upper Canada, Barrister at Law, Member of Parliament, Colonel of Militia, a Trustee of the U.C. Hospital and of the Central School, & c. & c. & c."

"Sir: Had you remained contented with the lucrative situation you hold in the service of the crown, added to the profits of your profession, and waited to take your turn for promotion amongst the rank of executive favourites, you should not have been now honoured with so prominent a place in the columns of a journal, which is intended not to contribute to the amusement of idle courtiers and sapient lawyers, but to the far more useful work of endeavoring to promote the public welfare.

Your notice to the people of Upper Canada that it is your intention again to obtrude yourself amongst their servants in the popular branch of the legislature, renders it, however, an imperative duty incumbent on all who love this country, on all who desire prosperity, to consider and scan your conduct in the last house of assembly, and from thence to determine how far you are deserving of the honours to which you aspire"....

"Thirdly - It is necessary to exhibit your want of economy, and lavish expenditure of the public money, (for all are agreed that you are very prudent and careful of your own.) Did you not propose 4000 dollars reward to Mr. Baby and Mr. John Macaulay for doing neither more or less than going to Quebec, staying a few days, assenting to some proposals of Mr. Hale and Mr. Morrogh, and returning to Upper Canada by stage and steam-boats. Was not Mr. Baby (who by the bye, as a private individual we greatly esteem) all the while in the constant receipt of his salary, &c. &c. &c. And has not Mr. Maccaulay places and offices, and Presidentships, and commissionerships enough? £100 was beyond the evident calculation of the expenses, yet you would have given them ten times that sum!! namely £1000. Did you act here on the good old principle that one good turn deserved another, or what was your motive?

In politics

>If thou wou'dst mix
>And mean thy fortunes be:
>Bear this in mind,
>Be deaf and blind,
>Let great folks hear and see."

This appears to have been your motto; you have been alternately the footstool and pincushion of power; you have retained that fawning cringing manner which is to the acute discerner, the most sure sign of political dependence and degradation.

You should have been the subservient tool of your schoolmaster and family patron, Doctor Strachan."

The effect of Mackenzie's new paper can be assessed by the reaction of Sir Peregrine Maitland, the Lieutenant Governor of the province, to the Advocate. At the laying of the cornerstone of the first Brock's Monument in 1824 a bottle with a copy of the paper was put inside. On hearing of it Maitland made the workers tear down the partially finished tower and the offending bottle removed.

Mackenzie's stay in Queenston was short. Before the year was out he packed up his family and moved to York where he would have a larger audience for his fight for self government.

HISTORICAL NOTE: The house of William Lyon Mackenzie in Queenston carries on the tradition of the early newspapers today. The Mackenzie Printery Museum is housed there with a collection of presses including the Roy Press brought to Niagara in 1792 by John Graves Simcoe. Volunteer printers bring this part of our heritage to life. For a great family outing visit the printery.

READ ALL ABOUT IT

The power of the pen did not reach the community that was growing along the Twelve Mile Creek until 1826. The Welland Canal was under construction and William Hamilton Merritt founded St. Catharines' first newspaper, The Farmer's Journal and Welland Canal Intelligencer. The paper, printed by Hiram F. Leavenworth, was published to promote the canal against its many detractors.

Many competitors sprang up in St. Catharines in the years following the opening of the canal. In 1832 the Mirror was founded by Joseph Clarke but ceased publication after only a few months. In 1833 the British Colonial Argus was published by J.H. Sears. A year later it was merged with the Intelligencer to form the British American Journal, which carried on the promotion of the canal.

One much travelled newspaper was the Niagara Mail. It began publication at Niagara in 1843. On May 28, 1851 the paper moved to St. Catharines under the ownership of Alexander Davidson and Eli McMullin. After less than a year in St. Catharines it moved back to Niagara where it continued until 1870.

Thorold received its own paper in 1849 with the founding of the Thorold Advocate and Welland County Intelligencer. A flurry of activity erupted in the newspaper business at the time of the Thorold paper. The St. Catharines Constitutional appeared in 1849 under John Giles. J. Richardson soon took over the paper. He ran it until 1854 when James Seymour became the publisher. The paper folded in 1871.

The St. Catharines Post began publication

September 13, 1853 as a semi-weekly. The editor was James A. Davidson and the paper advocated prohibition. The paper also was opposed to the union of Upper and Lower Canada under the Act of Union of 1840. It demanded the dissolution of the union. It gradually came out in support of the Reform Party led by George Brown, attacking Tories such as Allan MacNab and John A. Macdonald.

The Post changed hands twice in the 1860s. It became a weekly when John Murray moved his Thorold Gazette, which he had published since 1854, to St. Catharines and merged the two. It became a tri-weekly in 1866. The following year the paper was purchased by F. Munro, but by 1869 it was gone.

May, 1869 saw the birth of the St. Catharines Journal published by William Grant. The following year the Thorold Weekly Chronicle and Welland County Advertiser began publication under the direction of G.W. Hopkins.

John Graham started the Thorold True Patriot and Welland and Lincoln Reformer in 1866. On his death in 1870 the paper ceased publication, but quickly reappeared as the Thorold Mercury published by John McGovern. It folded in 1872.

The birth of the Canadian nation saw the advent of the St. Catharines Evening Star. The battle for readership with the Journal raged unabated from the beginning.

Two brothers, Richard and John Fitzgerald started the Times in 1868 selling out to P.E. Moyer in 1869. This paper lasted until 1876.

Eighteen Ninety-one saw the dawn of a new era in St. Catharines journalism. Deep in the throes of a recession, with empty store fronts staring out at passers-by on St. Paul Street, a new paper was launched to the disbelief of the business community and the competition. On April 21, 1891 The Daily Standard hit the newsstands.

Promoted by two Toronto journalists, George W. Miller and E.A. Hutchinson, the Standard promised columns that would be "bright and readable with local events of the day described as they occur in St.

Catharines and the Niagara Peninsula."

The publishers were quick to point out that, while the two rival papers supported the Liberal Party, the Standard was solidly behind John A. Macdonald and the Conservatives. The Standard was off to an auspicious start.

However, by early 1892 the bloom was off the rose. With mounting debts and the payroll in arrears, the two young journalists contemplated folding their grand expedition into the world of newspaper publishing.

The paper's mechanical superintendent was one William Bartlett Burgoyne. He had worked in the newspaper business as a printer at a number of papers throughout the United States and Canada and more recently at the St. Catharines Star.

This visionary of the press room saw the potential and approached Miller with the idea of buying him out. A relieved Miller set his price at $1.00 and Burgoyne owned half a newspaper. Hutchinson had also had enough and the Standard carried the following notice on February 3, 1892: "I have this day transferred to Mr. W.B. Burgoyne all my interests in The Standard newspaper of St. Catharines, Mr. Burgoyne assuming all liabilities and collecting all accounts due the said paper." It was signed E.A. Hutchinson.

With a dollar, a mountain of debt and the commitment of the staff, Burgoyne forged ahead to make The Standard an editorial and financial success. Henry B. Burgoyne, the publisher's son, was named manager of the job printing shop. The family tradition at The Standard had begun.

In 1908, the rivals Star and Journal merged to form the Star-Journal. It soon became known as just the Journal, but it could not compete against the community oriented

Standard and in 1920 the paper folded, leaving The Standard as St. Catharines daily newspaper.

The Standard began life on the second floor of the Saw Works on St. Paul Street. In 1898 it moved to its present location on Queen Street.

William B. Burgoyne acted as publisher of The standard until his death in 1921. His son, Henry took the reins and guided the paper through the Depression and the Second World War. He died in 1950.

A third generation of Burgoynes stepped up in the person of William B.C. Burgoyne. Bill had served overseas during the Second World War as an artillery officer. He guided the paper through some monumental changes in the post-war era. His untimely death in 1970 saw his sister Mary take the helm until 1972 when The Standard saw its first outside publisher in eighty years. Ross Bates, long time advertising manager, took the post until his death in 1975.

Another Burgoyne was waiting in the wings to take The Standard into the last quarter of the twentieth century. Henry Bartlett Burgoyne became the fourth generation of the family to run the paper.

In 1991 The Standard celebrated its 100th birthday. With the gobbling up of community newspapers by multinational corporations, we are indeed lucky to have a family owned newspaper that cares about our community. The Standard carries on the long tradition of the Niagara newspapers that have gone before.

If you walk down St. Paul Street some dark, misty night don't be surprised to hear the echoed call of a newsboy: "EXTRA, EXTRA, read all about it! Get your Standard here!"

CHAPTER TEN

THE UPPER CANADA REBELLION

As the year 1833 came to an end the situation at the Upper Canada legislature grew boisterous again. William Lyon Mackenzie was elected from the County of York and arrived to take his seat. His supporters crowded the gallery and raised such a din that the speaker ordered the building cleared of all spectators. The assembly denied Mackenzie his seat by a majority of four votes. William Hamilton Merritt was one of those who opposed his admittance. In his speech Merritt said, "I came down to the house yesterday to vote that Mr. Mackenzie should take his seat, but his conduct would have inducted me to vote him out of the assembly even if he had been a sworn member."

On March 6, 1834 another momentous occasion took place in Upper Canada. "Muddy" York became a city by an act of parliament and changed its name to Toronto. The first mayor of this new city was none other than the radical reformer, William Lyon Mackenzie. The stage was being set for the looming crisis of 1837.

While these events unfolded the dark clouds of rebellion gathered on the horizon of both Upper and Lower Canada.

The rebellion of 1837-38 was the result of political unrest that had festered since the 1790s. The War of 1812 had temporarily buried thoughts of reform beneath an avalanche of patriotic fervour, however, with the tardiness of the government in satisfying war loss claims opposition rose anew.

The main problem was the way the colony was governed. There was an elected assembly, but the actual governing was done by the Lieutenant Governor aided by an advisory body called the executive council that was appointed by him. The executive council and its supporters became known as the Family Compact because its members were chosen from the prominent Tory families of Upper Canadian society.

The unchallenged leader of the compact was the strong willed Anglican archdeacon of York, John Strachan. Strachan was a former schoolmaster who had taught most of the prominent men of Upper Canada at one time or another. His concept of the government of Upper Canada was a mirror image of England with the Church at its centre. By law the church was provided with valuable lands and political privilege. At the founding of the colony only the Church of England could solemnize marriages. Her schools and universities were meant to provide an intelligent clergy and an aristocracy fit to rule Upper Canada.

At the centre of this pending storm was William Lyon Mackenzie. As we have seen Mackenzie was a constant thorn in the side of the government. Through his newspaper, the Colonial Advocate, he railed against the injustices that he saw in society. He was chairman of several of the grievance committees set up by the elected assembly. The questions asked were often embarrassing. Why, he wanted to know, did it cost seven shillings to sent a letter to England? Why were the roads so bad between Toronto and Montreal that coaches could hardly get through? Did they know that bribery was rampant among election officials and that polling places were often held in the most inconvenient locations? Why were government contractors making so much money building the Welland Canal? Why were female lunatics chained together in the cellar of the county jail?

Mackenzie attacked his opponents at every turn, giving speeches wherever and whenever the opportunity arose. He could often be seen waving the red wig that he wore as he spoke. The stage was set for the greatest drama of his life.

The Legislative Assembly of Upper Canada was in an uproar in April of 1836. For the first time the elected assembly used its ultimate weapon against the governor and his executive council. It voted down the supply bill thus cutting off funds to the government. The Lieutenant Governor, Sir Francis Bond Head, countered by refusing to sign the bills passed by the assembly. An economic crisis followed causing severe unemployment sending many to the United States to seek work.

In July of that year the reformers were thoroughly trounced at the polls and even Mackenzie went down to defeat. It is said that on hearing the results he went to the home of a friend and wept uncontrollably. With this defeat the seeds of rebellion were sown and germination was not far away.

Mackenzie became a full time journalist again. On the Fourth of July, 1836, the sixtieth anniversary of the American Declaration of Independence, he founded a paper that he called the Constitution. In its pages he invited his fellow countrymen to join him in "this bold, dangerous, but delightful course," and in "preparing the public mind for nobler actions than our tyrants dream of."

He turned up the heat on the government with more vicious attacks than they had ever seen before. He wrote: "Tories! Pensioners! Placemen! Profligates! Orangemen! Churchmen! Brokers! Gamblers! Parasites! allow me to congratulate you. Your feet, at last, are on the necks of the people."

Somewhere in this period the seed of rebellion germinated in the soul of William Lyon Mackenzie. He was descended from the Mackenzies who had fought for Bonnie Prince Charlie against the English king in 1745. The ghosts of his rebel grandfathers rose up. The Clan Mackenzie was at war with England again. Mackenzie wrote: "Small cause have Highlanders and the descendants of Highlanders to feel a friendship for the Guelphic family. If the Stuarts had their faults, they never enforced loyalty in the glens and valleys of the north by banishing and extirpating the people. I am proud of my descent from a rebel race who held borrowed chieftains in abomination. Words cannot express my contempt at witnessing the servile, crouching attitude of the country of my choice. If the people felt as I feel, there is never a Glenelg who crossed the Tay and Tweed to exchange highborn Highland poverty for substantial Lowland wealth, who would dare to insult Upper Canada with the official presence of such an equivocal character of this Mr. what do they call him?-- Francis Bond Head."

As the chill winds of the beginnings of the winter of 1836 began to blow in Upper Canada the economic conditions became desperate. Jobs and currency became scarce to nonexistent.

Things worsened in the spring of 1837 when a general depression, brought on by the failure of several small banks in the United States, brought business to a new low. The country was seething with unrest, especially among the farmers who bore the brunt of the hardships.

Mackenzie lost no time in exploiting the situation. He predicted the return of brass money and wooden shoes, a reference to the days of the early settlers of the province. Banner headlines in "The Constitution" read: "EXCHANGE YOUR BANK NOTES FOR GOLD AND SILVER." The Bank of Upper Canada responded to the rush with shorter hours and one slow teller.

Mackenzie watched with hope at the situation in Lower Canada where the people were getting behind Louis Papineau and his call to protect the French language and culture. Early in 1837 Mackenzie decided to lay plans for a rebellion in Upper Canada.

The first step in his plan was to push the situation to the brink without actually going over the edge. A group of radicals met on the 28th and the 31st of July at John Doel's brewery at Bay and Adelaide streets in Toronto. The document they signed was just short of a declaration of independence. It praised the patriots' cause in Lower Canada and recited a long list of grievances. They established the Committee of Vigilance for the City of Toronto and made Mackenzie their Agent and Corresponding Secretary.

On August 3rd he went up Yonge Street to Newmarket and from there to Lloydtown where banners on the main street read: LIBERTY OR DEATH. An escort of fifty armed and mounted farmers took him on to Bolton for a rally. Mackenzie stormed on through the long hot summer despite threats of assassination. Mackenzie was in his element speaking from wagons and barrels.

Darkness fell on October 9, 1837 as Mackenzie gathered a hard core of radicals in the back of Doel's brewery. Jesse Lloyd, Mackenzie's contact with Papineau had arrived that day with an urgent message. The message: "The hour for a brave stroke of liberty had arrived. Would Mackenzie strike with the Patriots of Lower Canada?"

"Gentlemen," Mackenzie said, "The troops have left, Fort Henry is empty, and a steamer has only to sail down to the wharf and take possession. The governor is now home, guarded by one sentinel and my judgment is that we should immediately send for Dutcher's foundrymen and Armstrong's axe makers all of whom can be depended upon. We will march on Government House, seize Sir Francis, carry him to city hall, a fortress in itself, and seize the arms and ammunition there along with the old artillery at the garrison."

"We will declare a provisional government and send the steamer off to secure Fort Henry. If Sir Francis will not give the country an executive council responsible to a new and fairly elected assembly, we go at once for independence."

Mackenzie awaited their reaction. Dr.

Morrison, M.L.A., a former mayor of Toronto, shifted nervously in his chair when Mackenzie mentioned seizing the fort and the arms and muttered his disapproval. When Mackenzie had finished he indignantly proclaimed his opposition. The opportunity slipped by.

Mackenzie, however, was not to be denied and Thursday, December seventh was chosen as the day for the uprising. The date was an open secret and the government was warned, but Bond Head refused to believe that there was a serious threat to his government.

From there things moved quickly. On Saturday the second of December a warrant for Mackenzie's arrest was issued for the crime of high treason, a capital offense. Mackenzie was no where to be found by his desperate followers. In his absence Dr. John Rolph ordered the rising forward by four days to Monday.

Mackenzie finally arrived at the home of David Gibson on Sunday and ordered the original plan of a Thursday march to be adhered to. Despite this countermanding of orders the rebels began to march down Yonge Street armed with staves, pitchforks and rifles picking up reinforcements and Tory prisoners as they went. They began to gather at Montgomery's Tavern where news arrived that the rebellion was now general knowledge. There was no turning back now.

Things began to go wrong from the outset. The tavern had changed hands just a few days before and the new owner wanted cash for the promised supplies. Mackenzie ranted and threatened the new man, Lingfoot, to no avail. The men, tired and hungry, settled down for a miserable night. The Upper Canada rebellion was off to an inauspicious start.

HISTORICAL NOTE: Lord Glenelg was Secretary of State for the Colonies.

CHAPTER ELEVEN

THE BATTLE OF MRS. SHARPE'S GARDEN

Events moved swiftly as more men arrived at Montgomery's Tavern on the evening of December 2nd. Captain Anthony Anderson along with Samuel Lounts and Jesse Lloyd urged Mackenzie to launch an immediate attack on Toronto. Others counseled caution. Their men were tired, reinforcements were expected and John Rolph had not sent word as to the conditions in the city. Talk spread among the men of the militia being armed and of a contingent of Orangemen arriving in Toronto. The decision was made to postpone their march until daylight when all were refreshed and more reinforcements had arrived.

In Toronto, Colonel James Fitzgibbon, of Beaverdams fame, attempted to rouse Governor Bond Head to the danger that faced the government. In his nightshirt the governor listened to his military commander and then went back to bed having done nothing.

Fitzgibbon was determined to alert the city to its danger. He sent a young barrister's apprentice named John Cameron, a recent student at Upper Canada College, to ring the college bell. An irate housemaster stopped him after a few pulls of the rope.

The rebel guards at Montgomery's Tavern rested on their rifles as the initial excitement of the march gave way to boredom. The distant drumming of horses coming from the north brought them out of their malaise. Topping the little rise just north of Eglinton, three riders came charging down at the sentries. Ignoring the shouts to halt they went charging through at the gallop heading for Toronto. Rifle muzzles flashed and a prominent Tory from Richmond Hill, Colonel Moodie, rolled over the back of his mount, mortally wounded. One of the men with him was cap-

tured but the other made good his escape. First blood had been drawn in the Upper Canada Rebellion.

Alderman John Powell, along with a friend, moved up toward Montgomery's Tavern to see if the reports they had heard were correct. At the top of Gallows Hill Powell ran into Mackenzie with his patrol and was captured. Mackenzie asked Powell, as a gentleman if he or his friend were armed. With Powell's negative reply Mackenzie took him at his word and did not search them. On hearing of Moodie's wounding from the companion who had escaped, Powell pulled out one of his hidden pistols and shot Anderson in the neck killing him instantly.

Powell and his friend then charged down Gallows hill and overtook Mackenzie who had gone farther down Yonge street toward Toronto. He fired his pistol pointblank into Mackenzie's face. The priming flashed in the pan. The silence pounded in Mackenzie's ears. The powder in the barrel failed to ignite saving his life. Powell could only race off toward Government House to raise the alarm.

MacKenzie returned to the tavern and a council of war was convened where he urged an immediate march on the city. He pleaded and threatened but the leaders would not agree to act. Some wanted to disperse and they couldn't agree on tactics. This was all conducted with the groans of agony from a dying Colonel Moodie in the background. At midnight a light breeze blowing off the lake gave them their first news of Toronto. A faint tingling sound floated into the tavern as the men argued. Every church bell in the city was ringing.

Mackenzie finally assembled his ragtag army at eleven o'clock on Tuesday morning

to begin the march on Toronto. Mounted on a white pony and encased in several great-coats as if to ward off the Tory bullets that were sure to come his way, he led his troops down Yonge Street.

After a brief truce at Gallows Hill the advance resumed in two columns. The riflemen took the van with the pikemen, armed with twenty foot staves newly tipped with iron, following. Musketeers, with their fowling piece came next with the bulk of the army, men armed with pitchforks and beechwood clubs, bringing up the rear.

The column was a half mile south of the Red Lion when they came into range of an advance picket commanded by William Jarvis, the Sheriff of Toronto. It was ten passed six in the gloom of a cold December twilight. The twenty-seven men lay hidden in William Sharpe's garden and awaited the order to fire. The riflemen were within a hundred yards when Jarvis bellowed out the order.

The flash and the roar of muskets temporarily sent the rebels into confusion. Then two strange events took place. One should

have meant victory for the rebels, the second canceled out the first and led to the failure of the rebellion. After firing their initial volley the Tory picket, inexplicably, dropped their weapons and fled. The front rank of rebel riflemen recovered their composure and returned the fire from the picket. They immediately dropped to the ground to allow the men behind them to fire. This action was misinterpreted in the gloom as being caused by the accuracy of the fire from the picket. The riflemen in the second rank broke and ran back through the ranks of the pikemen sending the whole charging back up Yonge Street. The two sides ran away from each other as fast as their legs could carry them.

From her window Mrs. Sharpe watched over the corpse of a cooper from Sharon, the only casualty of the Tory volley. She watched through the night but none came to disturb the peace of her garden.

The morning after the battle of Mrs. Sharpe's garden Mackenzie attempted to rally the five hundred troop left at Montgomery's Tavern. Spirits were low however, and the deaths of two of the wounded men from loss of blood did little to encourage the farmers turned rebels. Yet they stayed on, still convinced that their cause was a just one. The rest of the day was spent by Mackenzie in robbing the western mail in search of information and harassing local Tories.

The following day the authorities in Toronto decided to act. At noon Sir Francis Bond Head, mounted on a stallion, led the militia up Yonge Street to the martial airs of two bands.

The rebel guards on Yonge Street saw the first troops come marching over Gallows Hill and raised the alarm. One hundred and fifty riflemen took up position in a wood and waited.

At the rattle of rebel musketry the first militia columns spread out in line on both sides of the road and advanced. Major Carfrae's artillery unlimbered and began to shell the rebel positions. Shot screamed through the trees to the accompaniment of the sound of falling timber. The rebels held their ground even as the artillery sang about their ears.

The appearance of a militia force on their left flank, however, drove the rebels out of the woods and the long retreat toward the tavern was begun. Once in the open the musketry of the militia started to take its toll and rifles were dropped as the men made a dash to the rear.

The rebellion was over. Mackenzie, along with other leaders, fled north to avoid capture. When Mackenzie looked back he could see the flames from Montgomery's Tavern shooting into the air. The governor had ordered it burned to the ground as the funeral pyre of what he called: "that perfidious enemy, responsible government".

THE EXILE

With the failure of the rebellion the rebel leaders split up and Mackenzie started for the American border in the company of a young lad of nineteen. His plan was to cross the Niagara River and make his way to Buffalo where he hoped to continue the struggle for the independence of Upper Canada.

Mackenzie entered the peninsula in the dead of night and sought out a friendly farm house. The nervous farmer gave them shelter and a meal. Here he left his companion who was suffering from cold and exhaustion. He pressed on arriving near St. Johns on Sunday morning pretending to be on his way to church whenever a patrol happened by.

He asked directions from a group of Methodists who put a patrol on his trail. He gave them the slip by turning up the road to St. Catharines and quickly doubling back to a friend's barn. He watched the armed riders thunder by. He had supper with the farmer and there met Samuel Chandler, a wagon maker. Chandler insisted on conducting Mackenzie to the border personally even though he risked the ruin of his family of twelve. To be caught meant the noose or transport to the Penal Colony in Australia.

They reached the upper Niagara River on Monday morning by walking through the night, dodging patrols every step of the way. On reaching the bank of the river they discovered that all the boats had been seized. Orders were also in effect that any Canadian boat in the water was to be fired upon.

Chandler managed to find a Captain McAfee who had lock his boat up in his shed avoiding the authorities. He offered to row Mackenzie across the river and his wife put a huge breakfast before them to prepare them for the journey. Before they could take a bite a patrol rode into sight, carbines at the ready. McAfee rushed to the shed and hauled the boat to the water's edge. The boat was just in the water when the patrol under Colonel James Kerby, collector of customs for the port of Fort Erie, rode up to the house to ask questions. Mrs. McAfee and her daughters engaged the colonel in conversation while her husband madly rowed Mackenzie out of range of the dragoons' rifles. McAfee steered for Grand Island and they were soon safe on

American soil.

Mackenzie arrived in Buffalo to a heroes welcome. He addressed the biggest rally the city had ever seen and true to form he whipped them into a frenzy of support for the cause of responsible government for Upper Canada.

One man in the crowd at Buffalo that heard Mackenzie was Thomas Jefferson Sutherland, who immediately pledged to follow Mackenzie in his quest. A friend of Sutherland's put out a call for contributions of arms and ammunition with the Eagle Tavern chosen as the collection place.

On December thirteenth Mackenzie crossed to Navy Island and declared a provisional government of a new Canadian Republic. Mackenzie raised the Patriot tricolour, with its twin stars for the two Canadas. As "chairman pro tem." of the new government he promised Canadian land and silver for every new recruit.

In true Mackenzie fashion he immediately went about designing a Great Seal. The first use of the seal, a new moon breaking through the darkness, was on a proclamation to all Canadians encouraging them to overthrow their oppressors and offering a five hundred pound reward for the bringing of Sir Francis Bond Head to justice for his crimes against the people. This notice was posted throughout the province. Of course the other prerequisite for the new republic was a printing press. Mackenzie cranked out stirring handbills for the oppressed citizens of Upper Canada.

The growing number of Sir Allan MacNab's militia patrolling the river bank south of Chippawa did not deter his resolve to continue. The Second Regiment of Lincoln Militia was called out and scoured the Short Hills near Fonthill searching for rebels. In June of 1838 the Mackenzie's forces did attempt to penetrate the Short Hills. A group of twenty-six men led by Samuel Chandler crossed the river and set up camp near Fonthill. The expected surge of disenchanted locals failed to materialize, but shortly after sundown on June 20, with their number now thirty-nine, they advanced on St. Johns.

They moved out in three groups hoping to pick more support on the way. The authorities were expecting trouble and the 13th Queens Lancers held the town. The rebels met at the common school and made their way toward the tavern on Main Street where the lancers were quartered.

A musket ball narrowly missed the sentry on duty, but it did awaken the other lancers. The rebels peppered the tavern with shot while the lancers defended themselves from the upper windows. They managed to gain the lower floor and threatened to fire the building with the lancers inside. The tavern was surrendered immediately. Initially the victors wanted to hang their prisoners in reprisal for the execution of two men in Toronto, but, cooler heads prevailed and the rebels rode off with their prisoners.

Word was quickly sent to the military and a hastily mustered troop of cavalry from St. Catharines hunted the rebels down. Samuel Chandler, wagon maker, of St. Johns, Benjamin Waite and a man named Moreau were sentenced to death. Moreau was hanged but the other two had their sentences commuted to transport to the penal colony in Tasmania. Chandler and Waite escaped from there in 1842 and the story goes that Chandler crept into St. Johns one night and took his family to the United States never to be heard from again.

In the meantime supplies poured in from American supporters who, perhaps, saw an opportunity to complete what they had failed to do in 1814. They chartered a steamer called the Caroline to transport food and munitions to the island. Mackenzie settled in for a long siege exchanging artillery rounds with the militia to ease the boredom.

The Caroline was almost the cause of a renewed war between Britain and the United States. In late December 1837 Colonel MacNab ordered his naval contingent to cut out or destroy the Caroline. At midnight the force shoved off with muffled oars to carry out their mission. The steamer was moored near Fort Schlosser and the party rowed under the stern to throw their grapples. There was a skirmish and one American was killed. The Caroline was taken out into the river, set afire and allowed to drift toward the falls. It broke up and sank in the upper rapids. The anger of the American public over this incident brought the two nations to the brink of war.

The American government wanted to avoid another war with Britain. Pressure was brought to bear on Mackenzie's supporters to stop their activities. When they attempted to buy another steamer at auction the local military authorities outbid them.

Two weeks after the destruction of the Caroline the rebels were forced to abandon Navy Island. The rebels did continue to raid Niagara through 1838 mainly as a pretense to rob the locals of their valuables.

Thus ended the Rebellion of 1837-38. Mackenzie was to live in exile for the next eleven years until pardoned by the government under the reformer Robert Baldwin. True to the Mackenzie legacy he was promptly elected to legislature and ended his years in the country he loved above all others.

CHAPTER TWELVE

THE FENIAN RAIDS

THE FENIAN BROTHERHOOD

In the aftermath of the American Civil War the Fenian Brotherhood's ranks were bulging with veterans of the victorious Union Army. The Fenians were founded in the 1840's to free Ireland from British control. An attempted revolt in 1848 failed and some of the rebels fled the country, many ending up in the United States.

The movement became organized in the United States in 1848. John O'Mahoney, one of the revolutionaries, arrived at New York and his writings and ideas were welcomed with open arms. The purpose of the society in America was to raise funds to equip the revolution back in Ireland. To give this revolution some impetus, the Irish Republic was declared, and a provisional government was established in the United States in 1863.

With the end of the Civil War a new scheme to attack Britain where she was most vulnerable began to emerge. The prevailing opinion among the Fenians was that Canada should be ceded to the United States as reparation for the cruise of the Confederate Navy's merchant raider, Alabama, which decimated American shipping during the war. She was built for the Confederacy in a British shipyard.

Canadian authorities were not idle while this posturing went on. Fearing an invasion on St. Patrick's Day they called up the whole of the active militia for immediate service on March 7, 1866. The British put their troops on alert as well with regulars stationed at several points, including Chippawa. When St. Patrick's Day passed without incident the militiamen were sent to their homes.

The plan to invade Canada split the brotherhood and led to furious infighting. The faction of the brotherhood under the head centre, John O'Mahoney, made plans to capture Campobello Island, a British possession off the coast of Maine. Their purpose was to set up a government on Irish soil by declaring Campobello a territory of the Irish Republic.

In the spring of 1866 the Fenian's ship, Ocean Spray, lay off Eastport, Maine awaiting orders. However, some zealous members, decided to land at nearby Indian Island and burn the store of a British subject, Henry Horton. The U.S. Navy immediately seized the Ocean Spray and the arms aboard her. The O'Mahoney faction never recovered from this fiasco.

Meanwhile, another faction under William Roberts continued to plan an invasion of Canada. Their general, T.W. Sweeney, who had been a Brevet Brigadier General in the Union Army, made his battle plan. Three thousand troops, the left wing of the Army of Ireland, were to land on the shores of Lake Huron, march on Stratford, and from there move on to seize London. The centre of the army was to advance in two columns, one from Detroit to help capture London and the other from Cleveland, which was to cross Lake Erie and seize Port Colborne and Hamilton. The right wing was to cross the frontier along the line of the St. Lawrence cutting communications between the two provinces.

Although hampered by the lack of funds Sweeney managed to buy ten thousand stands of arms from the United States Arsenal at Philadelphia and two million, five hundred thousand ball cartridges from the arsenal at Troy, New York. He established arms depots at St. Albans, Vermont; Potsdam, Buffalo, New York City, Cleveland and Chicago.

51

On May 10, 1866, Sweeney ordered all regimental property packed and ready for transportation. Late in May the Fenians began to move. Six railway carloads under the command of Patrick O'Bannon left Louisville, Kentucky, on May 27. The following day four hundred passed through Cleveland with colours flying.

From the beginning the invasion of Canada was beset with problems. The left wing of the army assembling in Chicago found only half of the three thousand men promised showed up. Even those that did come had no transportation as the officials of the Michigan Central, the Michigan Southern and the Northern Transportation Company refused to move the troops. The army of the centre could not find boats to transport them across Lake Erie and hurriedly moved their headquarters to Buffalo.

By May 30 several hundred Fenians were at Buffalo on the pretext of a convention. The following day many more arrived and, regardless from what direction they had come, they all told the same story: they were on their way to California to work on the railroad. Long into the night the conspirators met in secrecy in Buffalo going over last minute details. Secrecy was of the utmost importance if their plans were to succeed.

Although the headquarters of the centre of the army was still not in place, Sweeney decided to begin the invasion lest the element of surprise be lost. A mass meeting of Fenians was called for May 31 to cover up the preparations. As the meeting ended the men moved in a straggling line toward the Black Rock Ferry docks. Late that night one thousand men under the command of Colonel John O'Neill boarded canal boats, which were taken in tow by tugs, for the trip across the river. They had with them nine wagons loaded with arms and ammunition. The invasion of Canada was about to begin.

In the early morning darkness of June 1,

THE BATTLE OF RIDGEWAY

1866 the Fenian army approached the Canadian shore. The force of two thousand men with twenty-five hundred extra stands of arms with their ammunition landed at the Lower Ferry Dock, a mile below Fort Erie.

They immediately marched on Fort Erie and occupied the undefended town demanding rations for a thousand men from the reeve, Doctor Kempson.

A small force under Colonel Owen Starr was ordered to march along the lake shore to destroy a railway bridge. He was to take possession of the ruins of Old Fort Erie and raise the flag of the Irish Republic. The balance of the army then marched to Frenchmen's Creek and set up camp. They remained there throughout the day.

Meanwhile, the Canadian authorities were not idle. On the 31st of May the Queen's Own Rifles of Toronto received orders to embark on the steamer "City of Toronto" for the trip to Port Dalhousie, which they did in the early hours of June 1st. They proceeded from there by train to Port Colborne arriving there at 1.00 p.m.. They were later joined by the 13th Battalion from Hamilton, the York Rifle Company and the Caledonia Rifle Company. The 13th's Lieutenant-Colonel A. Booker took command of the force because of his seniority.

Another force was concentrated at St. Catharines under Colonel George Peacock of the 16th Regiment of Foot, a British regular unit . He moved his force to Chippawa on the first of June and occupied the village against a Fenian thrust in that direction. His force consisted of a battery of Garrison Artillery, the Grey Battery of Royal Artillery, five companies of the 47th Foot, two hundred men of the 16th Foot, the 10th Royals of Toronto and the 19th Lincoln Battalion. Peacock had seventeen hundred men under his command.

Peacock sent Captain Charles Akers, Royal Engineers, to Port Colborne with orders for Colonel Booker to proceed to a rendezvous at Stevensville. Colonel Peacock intended to march on the Fenians with his combined force.

General O'Neill, commanding the Fenians, decided to attack one of the forces opposing him before they could join up. On hearing that Booker was approaching Ridgeway he rushed forward and took up a position two miles from the town and waited.

Booker received information from local farmers that there were Fenians in the neighbourhood and immediately advanced in tactical formation with the Queen's Own in the van. The 13th Battalion, with the York Rifles formed the main body and the Caledonia Rifles followed up as the rearguard. The Queen's Own were equipped with the new Spencer repeating rifle, but the rest of the battalion still fought with the single-shot long Enfield rifle.

The Canadian Militia marched warily down the Ridge Road all eyes straining for signs of the enemy. A volley brought the advance guard up short and caused a few moments of confusion. The Queen's Own rallied and returned fire advancing as they went. The Fenians slowly gave ground and retreated to their strong position near lime Ridge.

As the fight continued the Queen's Own began to run low on ammunition. The 13th moved up and relieved them in good order and they continued to press the attack. The battle was going well for the Canadians when fate stepped in. A few Fenian horsemen appeared on the field and the cry, "Look out for cavalry," was heard. The order was given to form square giving the Fenian marksmen an excellent target. Booker quickly realized that no cavalry was present and tried to form line again, however, the initiative was lost, and he ordered the retreat. The Fenians had also had enough and began a rapid retreat back toward Fort Erie.

On arriving at Old Fort Erie, O'Neill discovered that a Canadian detachment of the Welland Canal Field Battery and the Dunnville Naval Company had captured some sixty Fenians at Fort Erie and were setting up headquarters there. An attempt to rescue his

men failed. As night came on the prospects of facing the British regulars that were most certainly on their way dwelled on O'Neill's mind. The American Navy steamer "Michigan" prevented any further movement from Buffalo and the Fenian position became hopeless.

O'Neill embarked his troops on an old canal scow towed by a tug and headed for Buffalo. As soon as they entered American waters they came under the guns of the Michigan and all were detained at the Black Rock ferry docks for four days. The Fenian invasion was at an end.

The casualty list for the Canadian Militia was ten killed and thirty-seven wounded. Once again Canadians had stood together to repel an invader.

The Fenians at Black Rock were released on promising to stay out of Canada. Twenty-two Fenian prisoners were taken to Toronto for trial and seventeen were condemned to death, however, these sentences were commuted. After serving prison sentence they were released.

Thus marked the last battle in the long history of the Niagara Peninsula. One year later Confederation brought the Canadas together as a nation.

CHAPTER THIRTEEN

IN SEARCH OF A NATION

While the Niagara Peninsula enjoyed the marvels of the Welland canal, railroads and suspension bridges, the broader picture of Canadian politics was coming to the fore. The 1850s was a time of peculiar political alignments. The Provinces of Upper and Lower Canada were united in the aftermath of the rebellions of 1837-38. A union resisted by Lower Canada, but finally imposed by London. The two Canadas soon became known as Canada West and Canada East, Upper and Lower Canada respectively.

The political deadlock that characterized this union brought together Sir Allan MacNab, the extreme Tory, and John A. Macdonald, the moderate conservative, who joined with George Etienne Cartier of Lower Canada to form the Liberal-Conservative Party. They were kept in power in the united parliament by their ability to keep the government running amid the turmoil.

George Brown, the fiery editor of the Toronto Globe and his Clear grits opposed the principle of double majority and advocated representation by population. Double majority said that in issues that affected one of the Canadas alone then a majority of the legislature must pass the bill as well as a majority of the representatives from the affected section.

The 1860s opened with the political situation in the United provinces running into stalemate. In the election of 1861 the Macdonald-Cartier government won a slight majority. The American Civil War was in full swing producing incidents between the United States and Britain. The government attempted to shore up Canadian defences by introducing the Militia Bill of 1862. The

French Canadian members balked at the half million dollar price tag and defeated the bill. The government resigned.

John Sandfield Macdonald, a moderate reformer from Canada West, teamed up with L.V. Sicotte of Canada East to form a government. They pushed through the Separate Schools Act for Canada West against the majority of members from Canada West precipitating the dissolution of the assembly. This government collapsed in 1864. Sir Etienne Pascal Tache and John A. Macdonald formed a Conservative government. It lasted just three months.

Four governments between 1861 and 1864 showed the futility of government in the United Province. Sectional conflict, racial and religious infighting and the practice of double majority all contributed to the problem. The government was at an impasse. Things had bogged down in political dissension.

At this point the Great coalition came into being. George Brown, Macdonald and Cartier's bitterest political enemy, persuaded the assembly to form a committee to look into the problem. Brown agreed to join with Macdonald and Cartier for the good of the country. Brown explained his actions this way: " . . . For ten years I have stood opposed to the Honourable gentleman opposite in the most hostile manner it is possible to conceive of public men arrayed against each other in the political arena . . . if a crisis has even arisen in the political affairs of any country which would justify such a coalition as has taken place, such a crisis has arrived in the history of Canada . . . party alliances are one thing and the interests of my country are another . "

While this was taking place the Maritimes

were discussing a union of their own. The government of Britain approved a Nova Scotia initiative to call a conference at Charlottetown, Prince Edward Island. Representatives from the Canadas were invited to attend. The march to Confederation was on.

John A. Macdonald stretched as he stepped from the train at Clifton. The member of the united parliament from Kingston had come for a meeting on the American side of the Niagara. Before doing so, however, he was determined to see the mighty cataract from Table Rock. After a brief lunch at the Clifton House he made his way by carriage to Barnett's Museum hence to the falls itself. Whispers among the people as to his identity soon gathered a crowd. So this was the man advocating a Canadian Confederation. Not one to pass up an opportunity to sell his ideas, Macdonald turned and addressed a few words to the crowd before moving off to his appointment.

William Hamilton Merritt struggled to keep his many enterprises afloat as the country marched resolutely toward confederation.

The Welland Railway Company, which carried cargo off loaded from ships to lighten them for the trip through the canal, was a constant drain on his financial resources. He went to England in an attempt to secure additional funds for the railroad. Hamilton's son William managed the family's business affairs in his father's absence. Lack of cash forced him to use the family's private funds leading to a seizure of the family home by the sheriff.

Merritt sailed for home early in 1860. He missed the steamer "Hungarian" on which he had booked passage due to a late business meeting. This turned out to be a fortunate occurrence for she foundered off Cape Sable with all on board. When he finally arrived at St. Catharines he found his wife ill. The stress of the loss of her home was a contributing factor to the state of her health.

In April Merritt took his place in the United Parliament. The seat of government and the forthcoming visit of the Prince of Wales were the main topics of debate. However, several important matters did come before the house. Hamilton voted for a dissolution of the Union of Upper and Lower Canada, but it was defeated. His attempt to get help for the Welland Railroad also met defeat. Except for a brief visit to Quebec to greet the Prince of Wales, this was Hamilton's last session of parliament.

While he was in Quebec his son William suffered a stroke and died on May 26, 1860. The death of his son greatly affected Merritt. The visit of the Prince and some traveling in the west did not shake the melancholy he felt at this loss.

Throughout 1861 Merritt pushed for the deepening of the St. Lawrence and other schemes to improve navigation on the Great Lakes-St. Lawrence route. Throughout this time Catherine Merritt remained in poor health. On January 10, 1862 she passed away.

Merritt set out in June for a trip to New Brunswick. While at Montreal he became seriously ill and the doctors indicated that he probably would not recover. He immediately set out for St. Catharines and home. He died on board the steamer "Champion" while it was passing through the locks at Cornwall. Thus passed from our midst the man to whom the Niagara owed so much.

HISTORICAL NOTE: John A. Macdonald visited Niagara twice before confederation. Once in 1855 for a luncheon at the Clifton house and again in 1866 for a meeting on the

CHAPTER FOURTEEN

OH! CANADA

American side of the river.

Excitement filled the air as the month of June 1867 wore on. A confederation of the four British colonies, Canada West, Canada East, Nova Scotia and New Brunswick had been proclaimed by Her Majesty, Queen Victoria, and all waited with anticipation for the great day. On that day as well, Canada West changed its name to Ontario and Canada East became Quebec.

However, not all waited with joyous anticipation . Many people opposed confederation bitterly. George Brown, the great Grit Reformer and editor of the Toronto Globe fought a hard battle against Sir John A. Macdonald and his dream of a Dominion from sea to sea. To him the proposed union smacked of American republicanism. As the rest of the country prepared to celebrate, a reform convention was in full swing at Beamsville. Even with union an irreversible fact, some thought to disrupt and harass the new government.

Newspapers on both sides of the issue flayed away at their opponents and at each other. In the peninsula the St. Catharines Constitutional was a strong supporter of Macdonald and confederation. The Welland Tribune on the other hand supported Brown and the Grit Reformers. One of Brown's supporters in the peninsula was Colonel J. A. Currie of the 19th Battalion. The St. Catharines Constitutional of June 13th, in announcing the holiday, took the opportunity to take a shot at Colonel Currie: "A general order has also been issued from the Militia department calling upon the volunteers to assemble at their respective headquarters on that day . . . We hope the various companies of the 19th Battalion will be brought together here in accordance with the order referred to; but we shall not be surprised if Colonel Currie's hatred of confederation prevents his taking any interest in the celebration . . . "

At twelve midnight, July 1st, the city of St. Catharines was awakened by the roar of the salute from Captain Wilson's Battery of Artillery. Canada was born! The artillery repeated the salute at seven a.m. and the day of celebration got underway. It seems that no formal program of festivities was planned in the peninsula, but, the St. Catharines Constitutional of July 4 gives us a glimpse of how that first Canada Day was celebrated: " . . . At 10 o'clock a fine company of volunteers arrived from St. Ann's to take part in the military movements. It seems they were under the impression that a general muster of the 19th Battalion would take place here; but in this they were disappointed. Only one other infantry company (Capt. Macdonald) and a few men from No. 3 appeared in uniform. These assembled on St. Paul Street at half past eleven and Col. Currie took command. Marching to a field in rear of the grammar school, where Captain Wilson's artillery and Capt. Gregory's cavalry were found posted . . . A "feu de foie" was then fired and three cheers given for the Dominion of Canada . . . In the evening there was a Strawberry Festival in Montebello Gardens under the auspices of ladies connected with the Canadian Presbyterian Church. The grounds were illuminated with colored lanterns and an abundant supply of strawberries, ice cream &c. was furnished at a small cost to all who wished to indulge in such luxuries, while the town band discoursed excellent music."

In Toronto, the capital of the new Province of Ontario, a grand military review took place. The first of July was declared a public holiday

to mark the birth of a new nation. Canada!

The Globe of July 1 described it as an up coming event like this: "At half-past ten a grand review will be held on the grounds west of Spadina Avenue. The volunteers muster at their headquarters at 9 a.m. and are expected to be on the ground in time to receive the general punctually at 10:30. The 13th Hussars, 17th infantry, two batteries of regular and one of volunteer artillery, Queen's Own, 10th Royals and Grand Trunk Volunteer Battalions, and Captain McLean's Fort Artillery company, will take part in the review. Line will be formed prior to the arrival of General Stisted, and immediately on his entry on the field a feu de joie will be fired by the infantry and a royal salute by the artillery."

At six o'clock in the morning a whole ox was roasted by Captain Woodhouse of the Barque "Lord Nelson" at the foot of Church Street. It took all day to cook and when it was finished a large portion was given to the poor of the city.

At nine p.m. fireworks were set off at Queen's Park. All the roads leading to the park were festooned with lanterns and bands played well into the night.

On July 8 a public meeting was held at St. Catharines town hall of the electors of Lincoln County to discuss the contentious issues surrounding confederation and the various factions for and against it. The St. Catharines Constitutional ran the story with the headline: "The new government sustained - Geo. Brown and his reorganizers condemned."

In the end the pro confederation forces won out and Canada proceeded down the road of nationhood. Some of the issues and arguments against a united Canada may sound familiar to us today. The problems that beset our country are not new, but, as in the past, we can only hope that the tolerance and goodwill that has always surfaced among our diverse ethnic groups will come to the fore once again.

INDEX